the Bible story

Heroes and Heroines

(From David's Victory Over Goliath to the Division of Israel)

VOLUME FOUR

the Bible Story

Heroes and Heroines ❖ Volume Four

Arthur S. Maxwell
Author of Uncle Arthur's *Bedtime Stories*

When Arthur S. Maxwell wrote *The Bible Story*, he used the King James Version of the Bible, closely following its narrative. This edition continues that tradition and draws from other translations using language that today's children readily understand.

NEWLY REVISED AND ILLUSTRATED

More than 400 stories in 10 Volumes Covering the Entire Bible From Genesis to Revelation

REVIEW AND HERALD® PUBLISHING ASSOCIATION
HAGERSTOWN, MD 21740

Illustrations not individually
credited are by Fred Collins,
Kreigh Collins, Russell Harlan,
William Hutchinson, Vernon
Nye, Paul Remmey, and
Herbert Rudeen.

Unless otherwise noted, all
Bible verses are from the *Holy
Bible, New International Version.*
Copyright © 1973, 1978, 1983,
International Bible Society.
Used by permission of
Zondervan Bible Publishers.
Bible texts credited to TEV are
from the *Good News Bible*—
Old Testament: Copyright ©
American Bible Society 1976;
New Testament: Copyright ©
American Bible Society 1966,
1971, 1976. Bible texts credited
to NRSV are from the New
Revised Standard Version
Bible, copyright © 1989,
Division of Christian
Education of the National
Council of Churches of Christ
in the U.S.A.

This book was
Revised by Cheryl Holloway
Edited by Eugene Lincoln
Cover art by Harry Anderson

PRINTED IN U.S.A.

R&H Cataloging Service
Maxwell, Arthur Stanley,
1896-1970
    The Bible story.
    1. Bible stories.   I. Title.
II. Holloway, Cheryl Woolsey,
1956-
            220.9505

ISBN 0-8280-0798-5

**Saul honored David for
slaying Goliath by
putting him over all his
fighting men. Jonathan,
the king's son, gave him
royal garments, and
they became lifelong
friends.**

PAINTING BY RUSSELL HARLAN

C O N T E N T S

PART ONE—Stories of David

PART TWO—Stories of the Shepherd King

PART THREE—Stories of Solomon

PART FOUR—Stories of Israel and Judah

PART ONE

Stories of

David

(1 Samuel 16:14-31:13)

The Lord is my shepherd; I shall not want. ✦ He maketh me to lie down in green pastures: he leadeth me beside the still waters. ✦ He restoreth my soul: he leadeth me in the paths of righteousness for his name's sake. ✦ Yea, though I walk through the valley of the shadow of death, I will fear no evil: for thou art with me; thy rod and thy staff they comfort me. ✦ Thou preparest a table before me in the presence of mine enemies: thou anointest my head with oil; my cup runneth over. ✦ Surely goodness and mercy shall follow me all the days of my life: and I will dwell in the house of the Lord for ever. --- Psalm 23.

David the Lionhearted

(1 Samuel 17:1-53)

IT WAS lonesome around the house. Three of David's older brothers had gone to help Saul fight the Philistines. Father and Mother were worrying about what might happen to them on the battlefield.

David was worried too. Out there on the hillside, looking after the sheep, he kept thinking about Eliab, Abinadab, and Shammah. Perhaps they would be killed or taken prisoners, and he would never see them again. That made him sad.

As he lay on the soft green grass, with the sheep feeding around him and the cool wind blowing over him, he wondered why people had to fight and kill each other. Then he remembered how one day a lion had come to attack his sheep, and he had fought and killed it all by himself. Would he ever forget that lion, or the bear that had tried to make off with one of his lambs? He hadn't wanted to kill them, but there was no other way to protect the sheep.

The Philistines were different. They should have known better. Why didn't they stay in their own country? Why did

9

As a shepherd boy, David faithfully tended his father's sheep. Alone with his flocks in the fields he learned lessons of God's love, and later wrote the beautiful shepherd psalm.

they have to come and bother other people?

Suddenly from far away came a familiar call.

"David!"

It was Jesse, his father. He wanted to send some food to the boys in camp. Would David please take it?

Would he! There was nothing he wanted to do more. Perhaps he would be there in time to see the battle. Maybe he would get a good look at the Philistines and find out what sort of people they were.

"Early in the morning David left the flock with a shepherd, loaded up and set out, as Jesse had directed."

We don't know how far he had to travel, but at last he came to the camp. He left the food with the man in charge, then searched among the soldiers until he found his brothers.

He was glad to see them again! But Eliab, the oldest, didn't give him a very happy greeting. Angrily he asked why David had come, and what was happening to the sheep he had left behind. "I know how conceited you are," Eliab said, "and how wicked your heart is; you came down only to watch the battle."

"Now what have I done?" sighed David, like any boy who has been scolded by an older brother.

Just then someone shouted, "Look, there he comes!"

David looked. To his amazement, a giant of a man, at least nine feet tall, wearing a huge bronze helmet, a bronze coat of scale armor, and bronze armor on his legs, came out of the camp of the Philistines. "His spear was as thick as the bar on a weaver's loom, and its iron head weighed about fifteen pounds [7 kilograms]" (TEV).

10

"Who's that?" asked David.

"Goliath of Gath," said someone, beginning to run away as the giant strode down into the valley which separated the two armies.

Why is everybody running away? wondered David. Why doesn't somebody stand up to this giant?

Disappointed and angry, he said aloud, "Who is this un-circumcised Philistine that he should defy the armies of the living God?"

Somebody heard what he said and told King Saul, who sent for David.

"Let no one lose heart on account of this Philistine," David said to the king. "Your servant will go and fight him."

Saul wouldn't hear of it. "You can't go," he said. "You're too young."

But David told the king about his fight with the lion and the bear, adding, "The Lord who delivered me from the paw of the lion and the paw of the bear will deliver me from the hand of this Philistine."

At last King Saul was convinced. This was a boy with the heart of a lion and strong in the strength of God. He told David he could go and fight Goliath if he wanted to, and he gave him a suit of his own armor to protect him.

Of course, the armor was too big. Nothing fit. David felt uncomfortable. "I cannot go in these," he said, and took the armor all off again.

Then, with his staff in his hand, he walked down to the brook in the valley and carefully chose five smooth rocks, putting them in the shepherd's bag which he carried.

What in the world is he doing? everybody wondered as they watched him calmly picking up one rock after another and judging them for weight and shape and smoothness. Is he just going to throw stones at the man?

They wondered even more as they saw him walk toward the towering figure of the waiting Philistine with no weapon but a sling.

As David drew nearer, Goliath became very angry and cursed him by the Philistine gods. "Am I a dog," he cried, "that you come at me with sticks? . . . Come here, . . . and I'll give your flesh to the birds of the air and the beasts of the field!"

David didn't pay any attention to this threat. Without a trace of fear, he replied in never-to-be-forgotten words: "You come against me with sword and spear and javelin, but I come against you in the name of the Lord Almighty, the God of the armies of Israel, whom you have defied.

"This day the Lord will hand you over to me. . . . The whole world will know that there is a God in Israel. All those gathered here will know that it is not by sword or spear that the Lord saves; for the battle is the Lord's, and he

12

will give all of you into our hands."

This was too much for Goliath. His face livid with anger, he lunged forward, his enormous spear grasped tightly in his massive hands.

Still David did not flinch. Instead, he calmly took one of the rocks from his bag, put it in his sling, and threw it with all his strength at the advancing giant. The watching thousands held their breath. Everyone knew there could be no second shot.

Suddenly Goliath stopped, stumbled, fell, his huge spear clattering to the ground. The rock had struck him in the forehead. Running toward the fallen Philistine, David grabbed the giant's sword and cut off his head.

The battle was as good as over. Seeing their champion dead, the rest of the Philistines fled in terror, the Israelites chasing them clear back to their own country.

How much God can do through one dear boy who loves and trusts Him with all his heart!

Winning a Princess

(1 Samuel 18:1-29)

THE DAY David killed Goliath was a turning point in his life. He never went back to his sheep. "From that day Saul kept David with him and did not let him return to his father's house."

For a while he was everybody's hero. King and people loved him dearly. Jonathan, Saul's son, took a great interest in the young shepherd boy, giving him "his tunic, and even his sword, his bow and his belt." This meant a lot in those days.

Young as he was, David was placed in "a high rank in the army. This pleased all the people, and Saul's officers as well."

Some boys' heads would have been turned by so much praise, but not David's. He behaved wisely, and "in everything he did he had great success, because the Lord was with him."

When he had returned from his successful attack upon Goliath, "the women came out from all the towns of Israel to meet King Saul with singing and dancing, with joyful songs and with tambourines and lutes. As they danced, they sang: 'Saul has slain his thousands, and David his tens of thousands.' "

This was too much for Saul. He began to feel jealous of David. He didn't like having the people say that David was 10 times as good a soldier as he was. The Bible says, "From that time on Saul kept a jealous eye on David."

The next day, brooding about what the women had sung, Saul suddenly became so angry that he threw a spear at David as he was playing a harp in the palace. Fortunately David saw the weapon coming, and dodged out of its way.

In spite of his jealousy, however, the king didn't forget his promise to give his daughter in marriage to the young man who killed Goliath. He couldn't. Too many people had heard what

he had said. Knowing how much they loved David, he didn't dare go back on his word.

But he cheated. "So when the time came for Merab, Saul's daughter, to be given to David, she was given in marriage to Adriel."

Saul sent word to David that he could marry his other daughter, Michal, if he would kill a hundred Philistines. He hoped that David would be killed in the fighting, but he wasn't. He came back alive and victorious. And now there was nothing Saul could do but give him Michal.

So the shepherd boy won a princess and became the king's son-in-law.

I wish I could say that they lived happily ever after, but they didn't. True, "Saul's daughter Michal was in love with David," but "Saul became still more afraid of him, and he remained his enemy the rest of his days."

It could have been such a happy family if only envy and jealousy hadn't spoiled it all.

Dummy in Bed

(1 Samuel 19:1-18)

NOW THAT David was married to Michal, you would think that King Saul would have forgotten all his unkind feelings toward the young man. But he didn't. Instead, he became more and more angry with him, and even told his son Jonathan to kill him.

That was the last thing Jonathan intended to do. He loved David and warned him of his danger. Then he went to his father and pleaded with him to spare David's life. He reminded Saul of how David had slain Goliath. "You were there," he said. "You saw it happen, and you were happy about it; why do you want to kill him for no reason?"

Jonathan won. Saul said he wouldn't kill David after all.

Very happy, Jonathan ran to where David was hiding and told him he could come back to the court and everything would be all right. So David returned and was given his old job in the army again.

For a while everything was peaceful, and David played music for the king as he had done many times before.

4-2

Then war broke out again with the Philistines, and David was sent to fight them. Once more he returned victorious, and once more, of course, everybody cheered him. Everybody, that is, except Saul. His old jealousy returned. He couldn't stand having the people say so many nice things about David. In a fit of rage he threw his spear at him again.

Fortunately the weapon missed him and stuck in the palace wall, but David thought it was time to go. Slipping out of the room, he hurried home and told Michal what had happened.

She was worried now. This time she felt sure her father would not change his mind. David would have to run away at once and hide. "If you don't run for your life tonight," she said, "tomorrow you'll be killed."

Even as they were talking, there was banging at the door of their house. David guessed it was Saul's soldiers, come to take him prisoner, maybe to kill him. What should he do? He could go to the door and fight them, but that might start a rebellion against the king, and he didn't want to do that. He could meekly surrender, or he could run away.

He made up his mind. He would leave. But how?

"The window," suggested Michal.

They opened it. The night was dark. David climbed out and let himself down to the ground. There was a whispered goodbye and he was gone.

Michal closed the window and quickly put an image in David's bed to make it look as if he were in it, fast asleep. Then she answered the door.

"He's sick," she said sadly to the king's messengers. "He's

18

in bed asleep; don't wake him up."

They demanded to see for themselves, so she let them in. There wasn't much light in the room. They took one look at the figure in the bed and concluded that if David was lying as still as that, he had to be terribly sick. Then they went and told the king.

Saul was furious. He ordered them to go and fetch David, bed and all. "Bring him up to me in his bed," he cried, "so that I may kill him."

The messengers obeyed. But when they went to pick up the bed, they soon saw how they had been tricked. "There was the idol in the bed, and at the head was some goats' hair."

What they said when they saw that dummy, we are not told. Maybe some of them laughed. But Saul didn't. He sent for Michal and gave her a real talking to for deceiving him.

She didn't mind. She knew that her father wouldn't kill her. And meanwhile David was safe, hurrying as fast as he could to Ramah to tell Samuel all that had happened. ✒

A Tale of Three Arrows

(1 Samuel 19:18-20:42)

DAVID might have fled to his home in Bethlehem and talked to his father and mother. But he didn't. He wanted to see the man of God who had anointed him. Life had become such a muddle. He had tried so hard to do right, and now all this trouble had come to him. He wondered why, and what he should do next.

"When David had fled and made his escape, he went to Samuel at Ramah and told him all that Saul had done to him."

It was a long story David had to tell, and Samuel must have been very disappointed at the way the king had treated this fine young man who had done so much for Israel. Just what Samuel said to David we do not know, but we can be sure he told him to be patient and to trust God to work everything out right in the end.

Not long after this, David met Jonathan again. They were so glad to see each other.

"What have I done?" David asked Jonathan. "What is my crime? How have I wronged your father, that he is trying to take

20

my life?" He couldn't understand why Saul would want to kill his own son-in-law.

Jonathan told him not to worry; he would let David know if there was any real danger.

But David was deeply troubled. "As surely as the Lord lives . . . ," he said, "there is only a step between me and death."

He told Jonathan what was worrying him now. It would soon be time for the New Moon festival (first day of the month), when the king expected everybody to be present. Maybe Saul would miss him and maybe he wouldn't. Yet he didn't dare go—not as things were now.

Jonathan promised to let David know what happened at the feast, "out of love for him, because he loved him as he loved himself."

They made a plan. David was to hide in a certain place near a field they both knew well. After the feast Jonathan would come to the field, shoot three arrows, and say to his arrow boy, "Go, find the arrows." If he called to the boy, "The arrows are on this side of you," then David would know that everything was all right and that the king had gotten over his fit of rage. But if he called to the boy, "The arrows are beyond you," then David would know that the king was still angry and he had better stay away.

Well, the feast began, and "David's place was empty."

Saul said nothing about it the first day, but on the second day he turned to Jonathan and asked where David was. "Why hasn't the son of Jesse come to the meal, either yesterday or today?" he asked.

He might have guessed if he had stopped to think how badly he had treated David a little while before. But he didn't. So Jonathan made some excuse about David's wanting to go to see his family in Bethlehem.

At once Saul suspected that the two young men had fixed this up together. "You perverse rebel!" he yelled at Jonathan, in front of everybody. "As long as the son of Jesse lives on this earth, neither you nor your kingdom will be established. Now send and bring him to me, for he must die!"

Now Jonathan was angry. "Why should he be put to death?" he cried. "What has he done?"

Trembling with rage, Saul seized his spear and threw it at his son. But his aim was bad, and Jonathan left the table "in fierce anger."

22

Early the next morning he went to the field with his arrow boy. Fitting an arrow to his bow, he said to the lad, "Run and find the arrows I shoot." And he obeyed.

When the young servant came to the place where the arrow had stuck in the ground, Jonathan called aloud, so that David could hear him, "Isn't the arrow beyond you?" Then again to the boy, but really to David, he called, "Hurry! Go quickly! Don't stop!"

The lad picked up the arrow and returned. Jonathan handed him his bow and sent him back to the city. When the boy was out of sight, David came out of his hiding place, and Jonathan told him all that had happened. Then they kissed each other and wept.

"The Lord is witness between you and me, and between your descendants and my descendants forever," said Jonathan as the tears rolled down their cheeks.

It was a sad parting. They both knew it would be a long time before they would meet again.

23

Goliath's Sword

(1 Samuel 21:1-10; 22:9-23)

THIS time David didn't go to Ramah. He went to Nob, where Ahimelech the high priest lived with his son Abiathar, who was probably serving jointly with his father.

When Ahimelech saw David, he sensed trouble. "Why are you alone?" he asked. He hadn't seen the other young men who had come with David.

David made some excuse about being on a secret mission for the king, and then he asked, "What do you have to eat?" The high priest must have wondered why, if he was on the king's business, David was so hungry. But he told David that all he had was the bread of the Presence, which was holy.

David said that that would be all right; he would take it if he could have it. "So the priest gave him the consecrated bread," five loaves in all.

Many years later Jesus told this story to the Jewish leaders of His day. When the Pharisees were finding fault with His disciples for picking heads of grain on the Sabbath, He said to

them, "Have you never read what David did when he and his companions were hungry and in need? In the days of Abiathar the high priest, he entered the house of God and ate the consecrated bread, which is lawful only for priests to eat. And he also gave some to his companions." From this Jesus drew the lesson that "the Sabbath was made for man, not man for the Sabbath." *

When David had eaten, he made another strange request. Was there a sword or a spear anywhere around that he could have?

Ahimelech looked at him in amazement. Imagine David without a sword or a spear! How could this be? David explained that he had come away from the court in such a hurry he had left his weapons behind, and "the king's business was urgent."

Usually, of course, there were no weapons in the tabernacle, but Ahimelech said he did happen to have something. "The sword of Goliath the Philistine, whom you killed in the Valley of Elah, is here; it is wrapped in a cloth behind the ephod. If you want it, take it."

25

David was delighted. "There is none like it," he said. "Give it to me." Taking the great sword from the priest, he hurried off with his companions to the city of Gath and took refuge there.

Unfortunately, one of Saul's servants had been in the tabernacle at the same time as David, and had seen and heard everything. "He was Doeg the Edomite, Saul's head shepherd." Later this man told the king how he had watched Ahimelech give David some of the bread of the Presence and the sword of Goliath. Greatly angered, the king sent for all the priests of Nob and accused them of plotting against him.

Ahimelech was shocked. He didn't know that there was any trouble between Saul and David, and he told the king so. "Who of all your servants is as loyal as David," he said, "the king's son-in-law, captain of your bodyguard and highly respected in your household?"

26

The king wouldn't listen. He was sure Ahimelech was lying to him.

"You will surely die, Ahimelech," he said sternly, "you and your father's whole family."

He ordered the guards to kill Ahimelech and all the priests who were with him. But the guards refused to obey him. They "were not willing to raise a hand to strike the priests of the Lord."

So the angry king turned to Doeg and told him to do this wicked thing. Being an Edomite, Doeg didn't care that these men were priests of the Lord, so he killed them. Then he went to Nob and killed all their women and children.

Fortunately Abiathar escaped. He fled to where David was in hiding.

You can imagine how David felt when he heard the news. He was terribly sorry and said, "That day, when Doeg the Edomite was there, I knew he would be sure to tell Saul. I am responsible for the death of your father's whole family."

But he added, "Stay with me; don't be afraid; the man who is seeking your life is seeking mine also. You will be safe with me."

So the two young men stayed together, trusting God to watch over them and to work everything out right for them in His own good time. 🖋

---

* Mark 2:25-27.

Song in a Cave

(1 Samuel 22:1-4)

FROM then on David lived a very hard life. He had no home anymore. He could not go to see his wife, for King Saul would have soon found out, and he dared not stay with his parents in Bethlehem, because that could have brought trouble to them. So he slept out in the forest or in the caves of the mountains.

One of these caves was called the cave of Adullam, and he stayed there for some time. His brothers came to see him, as well as the rest of "his father's household." Other people came, too. "All those who were in distress or in debt or discontented gathered around him, and he became their leader."

One by one they came to him, from all parts of the country, until he had a little army of 400 men.

It was a very rough group. Everyone had a grievance of some kind or other, and it would have been easy for them to become a band of thieves and cutthroats, stealing from the people throughout the land. But David let them know that wasn't his purpose. He told them about God, and many times

28

he sang about God's glory and love, as he had sung years before on the hillside while tending his sheep.

It was here, in the cave of Adullam, that he wrote that lovely song which later became known as Psalm 57. As you read it, think of the cave in which it was written, and of the four hundred men gathered around David as he sang to them.

"Have mercy on me, O God, have mercy on me, for in you my soul takes refuge. I will take refuge in the shadow of your wings until the disaster has passed. . . . He sends from heaven and saves me, rebuking those who hotly pursue me. . . .

"My heart is steadfast, O God, my heart is steadfast; I will sing and make music. Awake, my soul! Awake, harp and lyre! I will awaken the dawn.

"I will praise you, O Lord, among the nations; I will sing of you among the peoples. For great is your love, reaching to the heavens; your faithfulness reaches to the skies. Be exalted, O God, above the heavens; let your glory be over all the earth."

Try to picture the scene—the dark cave lit by a few smoky torches, the brave young man who killed Goliath, and his rugged newfound friends sitting and lying on the floor about him. In David's hand is a harp, which he plays as he sings the praises of God. Suddenly the cave becomes a temple, and sad, bitter men who have lost all hope feel hope and faith and love surge back into their hearts again.

About this time David did a very beautiful thing. Leaving the cave of Adullam one day, he went to see the king of Moab to ask a special favor.

"Would you let my father and mother come and stay with you until I learn what God will do for me?"

The king of Moab was friendly, and he agreed to the plan. So David went to Bethlehem and took his parents to the land of Moab, and they stayed there as long as David was in trouble.

How kind of him to remember his old mother and father and take them to a place of safety!

30

A God-led Life

(1 Samuel 23:1-13)

D AVID had a very simple faith. He took all his worries to God. Whenever he didn't know what to do or which way to go, he asked God about it, and God told him.

One day he heard that the Philistines were attacking the town of Keilah and stealing grain from the people's threshing floors. David wanted to rescue these people right away. But as he thought it over, he realized that in order to help them, he would have to leave the safety of the cave and go out where Saul might catch him.

What should he do? He talked to God about it. "Shall I go and attack these Philistines?" he asked. And God said, "Go, attack the Philistines and save Keilah."

When he told his men what he planned to do, some of them thought it wasn't wise. The danger would be too great, they said.

So David talked to God again. This time God said to him, "Go down to Keilah, for I am going to give the

Philistines into your hand."

So David decided to go and help Keilah. He now had 600 men, and together they defeated the Philistines and not only saved the people of Keilah but won back all their cattle.

You can imagine what a wonderful welcome he and his men received when they returned to Keilah after driving off the Philistines. But they did not enjoy it long.

While David and his men were fighting the Philistines, word reached King Saul that they had left their mountain hideout and gone to Keilah. Saul was sure he would capture David now. "David has imprisoned himself by entering a town with gates and bars," he said. So he called on Israel to go down to Keilah to besiege David and his men.

He forgot one important thing—that David was doing his best to walk with God and live a God-led life.

Somehow David learned what Saul was planning to do. Though there was no radio, television, or telephone in those days, the news got through to him. And when he heard it, he turned to God and asked, "Will Saul come down . . . ? O Lord, God of Israel, tell your servant."

God answered, "He will."

Then David wanted to know whether he should stay or flee. If the people of Keilah would stand by him and help him, he thought he might be able to win the battle. If not, he would be in very great danger.

So he asked God, "Will the citizens of Keilah surrender me and my men to Saul?"

Back came the answer, "They will."

32

Again David knew what to do. With his 600 men he left town and hurried back to the desert.

It is good to be able to talk to God like that. And God is as willing to talk to boys and girls today as He was to talk with David long ago. He will lead us all the way.

A Very Close Shave

(1 Samuel 23:14-28)

AFTER David and his men left Keilah, they went and lived in the desert strongholds and hills of Ziph.

Here David had a visitor whom he had not seen for a long time. It was his old friend Jonathan. Somehow the young prince had found out where he was and had taken the risk of coming to see him. How glad the two friends must have been to see each other again! And what a lot of things they had to talk about!

Jonathan was sorry for all the trouble David had been having. But he told him, "Don't be afraid. My father Saul will not lay a hand on you. You will be king over Israel, and I will be second to you. Even my father Saul knows this."

It was clear now what was the matter with Saul. He was afraid that David might become king someday, so he wanted to kill him and get him out of the way. But Jonathan was sure God was with David and that one day the kingdom would be his. How noble it was for the king's own son, heir to the throne, to say, "I will be second to you"! It takes a good deal of humility and grace to say that.

At last the two young friends had to say goodbye. "Then Jonathan went home, but David remained at Horesh." Jonathan must have traveled at night, for you can imagine what the king would have said if he had learned where his son had been.

But though Jonathan was friendly, the natives of the desert were not. Some of them, hoping to gain favor with the king, went and told him exactly where David and his men were living. Worse still, they offered to lead Saul's soldiers to the very spot. "We will be responsible for handing him over to the king," they said.

Saul was pleased, but he wanted to make quite sure. "Go and make further preparation," he said to these Ziphites. "Find out where David usually goes and who has seen him there. They tell me he is very crafty. Find out about all the hiding places he uses and come back to me with definite information. Then I will go with you; if he is in the area, I will track him down among all the clans of Judah."

This time Saul thought he really would catch David. The spies were certain they knew exactly where he was hiding. Since they lived in the desert, they thought they knew all David's hiding places. But smart as they were, they weren't quite as smart as David.

For when they led Saul's soldiers to the very spot where they were sure David and his men would be found, nobody was there. Desperately they roamed through the wild hills searching for them, but all 600 men had disappeared.

Once more, news of Saul's plans had leaked through to David, and he and his men had fled, this time to the nearby desert of Maon.

Of course, it wasn't long before Saul found out what had happened, and soon he and his soldiers were in hot pursuit. What a chase it was! For a while the two groups of men were so close that Saul's soldiers were on one side of a mountain while David and his men were on the other side.

At last David's band was completely surrounded, and there seemed no way to escape. "Saul and his forces were closing in on David and his men to capture them."

Then the miracle happened.

Suddenly a man appeared over the top of the mountain, running at top speed toward Saul's soldiers. Everybody who saw him knew at once that he was a messenger with important news.

"Come quickly!" he said to the king; "the Philistines are raiding the land."

The chase was over. Saul immediately called his men back from following David, and turned to meet the Philistines.

Once again God had come to David's rescue, and he and his men were saved.

Good for Evil

(1 Samuel 24)

DAVID and his men now enjoyed a little time of peace, but as soon as Saul returned from fighting the Philistines, he started off after his most hated enemy again. This time he took 3,000 men with him and went up into the desolate mountain passes "to look for David and his men near the Crags of the Wild Goats."

Day after day they searched, without success. The soldiers looked here, there, and everywhere, but they could find no trace of David or any of his men. They had vanished.

Saul was puzzled and annoyed. Where could they be?

One day he left his soldiers and walked into one of the many caves in that region. It was very dark inside, and the sudden change from the bright sunlight outside made it seem darker still. Saul did not see who was there.

Unknown to him, this was David's hideout, and the walls were lined with his men, all with their swords drawn, ready to fight to the death if they had to.

Saul was at their mercy, and David knew it. Some of the

38

men whispered to him, "This is your chance, kill him!" But David would not do it. He didn't hate Saul. He just felt sad that Saul hated him so much. Because he was the king, "the Lord's anointed," David would not hurt him.

But the temptation to play a trick on Saul was too great to resist. Noiselessly David crept forward in the darkness until he was so close he could have easily killed him if he had wanted to. With a quick slash of his dagger, he cut off part of Saul's garment and carried it back to his men.

Then he wished he hadn't done it. The Bible says that "David was conscience-stricken for having cut off a corner of his robe. He said to his men, 'The Lord forbid that I should do such a thing to my master, the Lord's anointed.' " But he couldn't put it back.

Saul had no idea of what had just happened to him. He walked out of the cave and headed toward his soldiers, who were waiting for him not far away. Suddenly he heard a shout behind him.

"My lord the king!"

Startled, he turned, and saw David bowing humbly before him.

For a moment Saul did not know what to say or do. Then David called to him in a tender, pleading voice, "Why do you listen when men say, 'David is bent on harming you'? . . . You have seen with your own eyes how the Lord delivered you into my hands in the cave. Some urged me to kill you, but I spared you; I said, 'I will not lift my hand against my master, because he is the Lord's anointed."

Then he held up the piece of cloth.

"My father," he said, "look at this piece of your robe in my hand! I cut off the corner of your robe but did not kill you. Now understand and recognize that I am not guilty of wrongdoing or rebellion. . . . May the Lord be our judge and decide between us. May he consider my cause and uphold it; may he vindicate me by delivering me from your hand."

Saul's heart was touched. He began to weep.

" 'Is that your voice, David my son? . . . You are more righteous than I,' he said. 'You have treated me well, but I have treated you badly.' "

They talked together for some time, as friendly as in the happy days gone by. Then they said goodbye. Saul took his soldiers back home with him, and David and his men returned to their cave.

There was no fighting that day. Nobody was killed and nobody was hurt. People can't fight when somebody returns good for evil as David did.

Brave, Beautiful Abigail

(1 Samuel 25:1-42)

I T MUST have been hard for David to find food for his 600 men. They couldn't live forever on the plants and berries they found in the woods, or even on the birds and wild animals they were able to shoot with their bows and arrows. Now and then they had to ask farmers to help them.

Of course, they could have taken food without asking for it, but that was not David's way. He was not a thief or a bandit. He always remembered that he had been anointed by the prophet of the Lord as the future king of Israel.

One day he sent 10 of his young men to ask for food from a very wealthy farmer named Nabal. This man owned 3,000 sheep and 1,000 goats, which was a lot of animals in those days. David had helped to protect his flocks and had good reason to expect something in return. But Nabal was as mean as he was rich.

"Long life to you! Good health to you and your household! And good health to all that is yours!" said the young men courteously, as they told Nabal what David wanted.

But Nabal happened to be in a very bad mood. "Who is this David?" he snarled. "And who is this son of Jesse? Many servants are breaking away from their masters these days. Why should I take my bread and water, and the meat I have slaughtered for my shearers, and give it to men coming from who knows where?"

He wouldn't give a loaf of bread, a drop of water, or a single kid to David, and he sent the young men away empty-handed.

Now it was David's turn to get angry. He had never met such meanness before and couldn't take it. He ordered 400 of his men to follow him to Nabal's farm, planning to punish the man for his rudeness and selfishness.

But he didn't need to get so stirred up. God was still working things out for him as He always had before.

Nabal's wife happened to be a very wise woman, as well as beautiful and brave. The servants told her how Nabal had treated David's 10 messengers, and she became upset. When she learned that David's men had been protecting both her shepherds and her sheep, she wanted to do something to make things right.

Without saying a word to Nabal, she "lost no time. She took two hundred loaves of bread, two skins of wine, five dressed sheep, five seahs of roasted grain, a hundred cakes of raisins and two hundred cakes of pressed figs, and loaded them on donkeys." She knew all this food would be a wonderful feast for men who had been living on desert rations for such a long time.

Abigail wisely sent her servants ahead with the food-laden

donkeys, while she rode behind. Perhaps she remembered how Jacob had once sent presents ahead of him to appease his brother Esau.

When she was partway down the hillside trail, she ran right into David and his men. In a moment they surrounded her and her servants.

The sight of all these fierce-looking men was enough to frighten anybody, certainly a lone woman. But not Abigail. She had expected something like this to happen and was ready for it. Calmly she got off her donkey and bowed respectfully to David.

Then she pointed to all the food and explained how this was a present she had brought for his young men.

Anger melted away. Smiles broke out on the faces of those 400 men at the thought of the wonderful meal they would soon enjoy.

"Please, don't pay any attention to Nabal," she said to David. "He is exactly what his name means—a fool" (TEV).

Then, very sweetly, she took all the blame for the misunderstanding upon herself. "Please forgive your servant's offense," she said.

What could David do? His heart was touched. He couldn't go and punish this lovely woman's husband now. She was just too sweet and beautiful, and so very gracious!

"Praise be to the Lord, the God of Israel," he said to her, "who has sent you today to meet me. May you be blessed for your good judgment and for keeping me from bloodshed this day."

Everybody was happy now. Eagerly the men took the food off the donkeys, and with many thanks went back the way they had come.

Abigail returned home, and finding her husband drunk, told him nothing about what she had done until the morning. When she finally broke the news to him, he was so shocked he had a stroke and died a few days later.

When news of Nabal's death reached David, he said, "Praise be to the Lord. . . . He has kept his servant from doing wrong and has brought Nabal's wrongdoing down on his own head."

David had admired Abigail, the brave woman who had dared to come alone to meet him when he was angry. He sent messengers to invite her to come and live with him in the desert. Gladly she said Yes and became his wife. 🖋

45

avid blessed the Lord when Abigail, wife of
icked Nabal, in return for protection of her
ısband's herds, brought food to David's
ur hundred hungry men in the wilderness.

Night Adventure

(1 Samuel 26:1-27:4)

ONE DAY, when David was back in the Desert of Ziph, he heard that Saul was coming after him. He could hardly believe his ears. After what had happened at the cave, when he and the king had had such a friendly chat together, he had thought there would be no more trouble between them. But now Saul was chasing him again.

To make quite sure the story was true, "David . . . sent out scouts and learned that Saul had definitely arrived."

Saddened by the news, David wrote the beautiful prayer now found in Psalm 54: "Save me, O God, by your name; vindicate me by your might. Hear my prayer, O God; listen to the words of my mouth. . . . Surely God is my help; the Lord is the one who sustains me. . . . I will sacrifice a freewill offering to you; I will praise your name, O Lord, for it is good."

This time David and his men did not run away. Instead, in the middle of the night, they crept toward the place where Saul and his soldiers were camped.

Closer and closer they moved until they could make out

the very place where Saul and Abner, his chief commander, were sleeping. Saul, they noticed, was in the center of the camp, in the middle of the supplies. Abner was near him, while the rest of the soldiers lay on the ground all around them.

Everyone was fast asleep. Not a sound was to be heard except for the snoring of some of the soldiers and the occasional braying of a donkey. Suddenly David whispered to two of his bravest men, "Who will go down into the camp with me to Saul?"

"I will," said Abishai.

Without a thought of the terrible risk they were taking, the two brave men crept forward. What if a dog barked? What if a sentinel saw them? If they woke the camp, they wouldn't stand a chance. On they went, careful not to step on any of the sleeping soldiers.

At last they found Saul, sound asleep. Beside him was his spear, stuck in the ground, and a bottle of water.

As Abishai looked down at the man who had given

David and his men so much trouble he longed to kill him then and there. "Let me pin him to the ground with one thrust of my spear," he whispered to David. "I won't strike him twice."

But David would not let him do it. "Don't destroy him!" he said, "Who can lay a hand on the Lord's anointed and be guiltless? As surely as the Lord lives, . . . the Lord himself will strike him; either his time will come and he will die, or he will go into battle and perish."

Once more he showed his faith in God's leading of his life. Then, with the same trace of mischief which he had shown in the cave when he cut off part of Saul's garment, he whispered to Abishai, "Now get the spear and water jug that are near his head, and let's go."

As silently as they had come, the two men crept out of the camp. "Then David crossed over to the other side and stood on top of the hill some distance away; there was a wide space between them."

It must have been very early in the morning, because when

48

he shouted, nobody answered. Everybody in the camp was still asleep.

Then he called again across the valley, at the top of his voice, "Aren't you going to answer me, Abner?"

Abner got up, very much out of sorts. "Who are you who calls to the king?" he roared.

"You're a man, aren't you?" taunted David. "And who is like you in Israel? Why didn't you guard your lord the king? Someone came to destroy your lord the king. . . . Look around you. Where are the king's spear and water jug that were near his head?"

"Who is it?" I can hear Abner muttering. "What's he talking about?"

But Saul knew David's voice, and called back, "Is that your voice, David my son?"

"Yes it is, my lord the king," David said. Then he asked the question he had asked so many times before, "What have I done, and what wrong am I guilty of?"

When Saul saw his spear and the jug of water in David's hands, and realized that David must have been by his bed that night, he said, "I have sinned. Come back, David my son. Because you considered my life precious today, I will not try to harm you again. Surely I have acted like a fool and have erred greatly."

That was the truest thing Saul ever said. The pity was, he said it too late.

David, as ready as ever to forgive, called back, "Here is the king's spear. . . . Let one of your young men come over and get it."

The king was grateful. "May you be blessed, my son David," he said. "You will do great things and surely triumph."

It was a happy ending to a long quarrel.

David and his men went to Gath, and Saul "no longer searched for him."

The Witch of Endor

(1 Samuel 28)

ONE REASON why Saul stopped searching for David was because the Philistines were invading the country again. This time they had a huge army, and when Saul saw them "he was afraid; terror filled his heart."

He needed advice but didn't know where to go to get it. Other times when he was in trouble he had gone to Samuel, who had always given him advice from the Lord. But now Samuel was dead.

He would have liked to ask the high priest, but he was dead too. Saul had ordered Doeg to kill all the priests, and only Abiathar had escaped. But he had fled to David for refuge because he was afraid of Saul's anger.

Saul had never felt so lonely and helpless before. He prayed to God, but because of his disobedience, "the Lord would not answer him."

As the Philistines drew nearer Saul became desperate. At

51

last he decided to go to a witch and ask her to help him. It was the worst thing he could have done.

In those days a woman who claimed to be able to talk with the dead was called a witch. Because this claim was false, God had said that all witches should not be allowed to live in the land. While Samuel was alive Saul had tried to get rid of them, but a few were still left.

Learning that one of these women lived at a place called Endor, the king disguised himself in common clothes and went to visit her with two of his friends.

It was night when they arrived, and the witch was afraid

that they might be spies who would betray her. But Saul promised solemnly that no one would hurt her if she did what he asked.

"Whom shall I bring up for you?" asked the woman.

"Bring up Samuel," he said.

Of course she couldn't do that. The figure she said she saw was not Samuel but an evil spirit that looked like Samuel.

As for Saul, he didn't see Samuel. He just believed what the woman told him. Thinking he was talking to Samuel, he said, "I am in great distress. . . . The Philistines are fighting against me, and God has turned away from me. He no longer answers me, either by prophets or by dreams. So I have called on you to tell me what to do."

If Saul thought that he was going to get some good advice or some encouraging word, he was mistaken. The voice that spoke to him, claiming to be the voice of Samuel, had nothing but bad news. Israel, it said, would be defeated in the battle with the Philistines, and Saul and his sons would be killed.

Saul came away from the witch of Endor completely discouraged. He had received no help at all. And now he had no heart to fight the Philistines and no strength to plan the war against them. Without hope and without God, he could only wait for the disaster he knew was coming.

53

← PAINTING BY VERNON NYE

Saul's disobedience went so far that when surrounded by the Philistines he sought the counsel of a witch who brought up an evil spirit that pretended he was Samuel the prophet.

Gallant Rescue

(1 Samuel 29:1-30:25)

DAVID was having his share of trouble too. King Achish of Gath had been very kind to him and his men, and had let them make their home in the little town of Ziklag. Happy to have a place of their own at last, the 600 men, with their wives and children, had built up the town and made it prosperous.

Then came the new war between the Philistines and Israel. This was bad for David, because Ziklag and Gath were in the land of the Philistines, and King Achish expected to use all his able-bodied men in the fight against Israel.

But how could David fight against his own people? He and his men must have talked over the problem a long time. The Bible doesn't tell us what they decided to do. We just know that when all the soldiers gathered for the attack, and "the Philistine rulers marched with their units of hundreds and thousands, David and his men were marching at the rear with Achish."

54

Suddenly some commanders of the Philistines noticed them. "What about these Hebrews?" they demanded.

King Achish told them not to worry. David and his men had been living with him for a long time, he said, and he had never had a problem with them.

But the commanders would not hear of Hebrews fighting in their ranks against Israel. Angrily pointing at David, they said, "Send the man back. . . . He must not go with us into battle, or he will turn against us during the fighting."

They had a point, and Achish saw it. He called David and begged him to return to Ziklag. "I know that you have been as pleasing in my eyes as an angel of God; nevertheless, the Philistine commanders have said, 'He must not go up with us into battle.' Now get up early, along with your master's servants who have come with you, and leave in the morning as soon as it is light."

There was nothing else David could do. He and his men left for home. And it was a good thing they did. When they got back to Ziklag, they found it burned to the ground.

The Amalekites had attacked the city while the men were all away and had carried off the women and children and everything David and his men possessed.

It was a terrible shock. They had never dreamed that anything like this would ever happen to them. "So David and his men wept aloud until they had no strength left to weep."

55

What a sad, sad day that was! But the men were not only sad, they were angry. Some said that David ought to be stoned, as though it were all his fault. "But David found strength in the Lord his God."

Standing among the charred ruins of the city, he said to God, "Shall I pursue this raiding party? Will I overtake them?"

"Pursue them," God said to him. "You will certainly overtake them and succeed in the rescue."

David and his men set off after the Amalekites. They drove themselves so hard that by the time they reached the Besor Ravine, 200 of them were so tired they couldn't go a step farther. These men were left behind with the supplies at the ravine while the rest hurried on.

As David's men followed the Amalekite's trail, they found a young Egyptian lying in a field. He was sick and weak with hunger, so they gave him some figs and raisins to eat. Pretty soon he was feeling well enough to talk. He said he was a servant of one of the Amalekites who had burned Ziklag. On the way back he had fallen ill, and his master had left him. He told David which way the Amalekites had gone.

This was good news, and soon the 400 men were on their way again. That evening they caught up with the enemy, and what a sight they saw! The Amalekites were "scattered over the countryside, eating, drinking and reveling because of the great amount of plunder they had taken from the land of the Philis-

57

← PAINTING BY VERNON NYE

While pursuing the Amalekites, David found a sick slave boy left by his master to die on the field. He comforted the lad with food, and the boy told which way the enemy had gone.

The next day, when the battle was over and the Philistines began to strip the slain, they came across the bodies of Saul and his three sons.

"They cut off his head and stripped off his armor, and they sent messengers throughout the land of the Philistines to proclaim the news in the temple of their idols and among their people."

Later they fastened his body to the wall of the city of Beth Shan. "They put his armor in the temple of their gods and hung up his head in the temple of Dagon."

It was a terrible end for one who had once been chosen by God to be the first king of Israel. Why did he die?

The Bible says that "Saul died because he was unfaithful to the Lord; he did not keep the word of the Lord and even consulted a medium for guidance."

So it was really disobedience that caused his death. Time and again he had disobeyed God, and finally his wrongdoing caught up with him. In going to the witch of Endor he went just one step too far.

Disobeying God is always dangerous. Of course, if we repent and tell Him we are sorry, He will forgive us. But if we go on and on doing things He has told us not to do, the day will come when we may suffer a fate as sad as Saul's.

The next day, when the battle was over and the Philistines began to strip the slain, they came across the bodies of Saul and his three sons.

"They cut off his head and stripped off his armor, and they sent messengers throughout the land of the Philistines to proclaim the news in the temple of their idols and among their people."

Later they fastened his body to the wall of the city of Beth Shan. "They put his armor in the temple of their gods and hung up his head in the temple of Dagon."

It was a terrible end for one who had once been chosen by God to be the first king of Israel. Why did he die?

The Bible says that "Saul died because he was unfaithful to the Lord; he did not keep the word of the Lord and even consulted a medium for guidance."

So it was really disobedience that caused his death. Time and again he had disobeyed God, and finally his wrongdoing caught up with him. In going to the witch of Endor he went just one step too far.

Disobeying God is always dangerous. Of course, if we repent and tell Him we are sorry, He will forgive us. But if we go on and on doing things He has told us not to do, the day will come when we may suffer a fate as sad as Saul's.

Saul's Sad End

(1 Samuel 31; 1 Chronicles 10)

NOT LONG after Saul went to see the witch of Endor, he found himself at the head of his army facing the Philistines. It was a bad day for Israel. Right from the start the battle was as good as lost. There wasn't a chance of victory when the king himself was discouraged. Knowing God was no longer with him, he expected to be defeated, and he was.

Hardly had the fight begun when "the Israelites fled before them." Saul and his sons fled too, with the Philistines hard after them. First Jonathan was killed, then his two brothers.

Shortly afterward an arrow struck Saul, wounding him badly. Certain that his end was near, he asked his armor-bearer to kill him. When he would not do it, "Saul took his own sword and fell on it" and killed himself. Then the armor-bearer, seeing his master was dead, "fell on his sword and died with him."

tines and from Judah." In the middle of the drunken soldiers, they saw their wives and children, some of them no doubt tied up as prisoners.

At dawn the next day, (TEV), David gave the order to attack, and the 400 men dashed to the rescue of their loved ones. They fought the Amalekites furiously "from dusk until the evening of the next day."

How the children must have shouted for joy when they saw their fathers coming to save them! I can almost hear them crying, "Look, Mamma, there's Daddy come to rescue us!"

When the fight was over there was a wonderful reunion as husbands and wives, brothers and sisters, hugged each other. Everybody was saved. "David recovered everything"—all the mothers, all the children, all the flocks, and all the herds, just as God had promised.

For a little while everybody was wildly happy. Then a big argument began. Some of the men who had gone with David and done the fighting said that the others who had stayed behind at the ravine had no right to any of the plunder, except that "each man may take his wife and children."

But David would have none of it. There was no littleness or meanness in his heart. "You must not do that with what the Lord has given us," he said. "The share of the man who stayed with the supplies is to be the same as that of him who went down to the battle. All will share alike."

And so they did.

58

GALLANT RESCUE

What a sad, sad day that was! But the men were not only sad, they were angry. Some said that David ought to be stoned, as though it were all his fault. "But David found strength in the Lord his God."

Standing among the charred ruins of the city, he said to God, "Shall I pursue this raiding party? Will I overtake them?"

"Pursue them," God said to him. "You will certainly overtake them and succeed in the rescue."

David and his men set off after the Amalekites. They drove themselves so hard that by the time they reached the Besor Ravine, 200 of them were so tired they couldn't go a step farther. These men were left behind with the supplies at the ravine while the rest hurried on.

As David's men followed the Amalekite's trail, they found a young Egyptian lying in a field. He was sick and weak with hunger, so they gave him some figs and raisins to eat. Pretty soon he was feeling well enough to talk. He said he was a servant of one of the Amalekites who had burned Ziklag. On the way back he had fallen ill, and his master had left him. He told David which way the Amalekites had gone.

This was good news, and soon the 400 men were on their way again. That evening they caught up with the enemy, and what a sight they saw! The Amalekites were "scattered over the countryside, eating, drinking and reveling because of the great amount of plunder they had taken from the land of the Philis-

57

While pursuing the Amalekites, David found a sick slave boy left by his master to die on the field. He comforted the lad with food, and the boy told which way the enemy had gone.

PART TWO

Stories of

the Shepherd King

(2 Samuel 1:1-24:25; 1 Chronicles 1:1-21:30)

Man With a Crown

(2 Samuel 1)

D AVID had been back in Ziklag only two days after his victory over the Amalekites when on the third day news reached him about Saul's death.

Everybody in the burned-out city had been too busy clearing things up and sorting out the goods they had taken from the Amalekites to give a thought to what might have happened in the Philistine battle with Israel. Then a messenger came whose news changed all their lives.

David took one glance at him and guessed that he brought bad news, because his clothes were torn and there was dirt on his head.

"What happened?" David asked him.

Then the man told his story. He had been on Mount Gilboa when Saul was running from the Philistines and had seen the chariots closing in on him. Then, he said, Saul had called to him and begged, "Stand over me and kill me! I am in the throes of death, but I'm still alive."

"So," the messenger said, "I stood over him and killed

63

The soldier who brought Saul's crown and bracelet to David as proof he had slain the king was surprised when David turned on him for taking the life of the Lord's anointed.

him, because I knew that after he had fallen he could not survive. And I took the crown that was on his head and the band on his arm and have brought them here to my lord."

Then he produced the royal regalia and handed it to David. How everybody must have stared at that crown!

The messenger probably thought David would give him a lot of money for his boast that he had killed Saul, but he was mistaken. There was no happiness in Ziklag that day or any rejoicing over a fallen enemy. Everybody "mourned and wept and fasted till evening for Saul and his son Jonathan, and for the army of the Lord and the house of Israel, because they had fallen by the sword."

The messenger couldn't understand it. Why all this weeping? he wondered. Hadn't he brought good news? But he had another surprise coming.

Angrily David turned on him, demanding to know why he was not afraid to destroy the Lord's anointed. To David killing the king was a terrible crime.

"Go, strike him down," he ordered, and one of his young men killed the man on the spot.

Then David, always the poet, wrote these lines about Saul and Jonathan whom he had loved so much:

"Your glory, O Israel, lies slain on your heights. How the mighty have fallen!

"Tell it not in Gath, proclaim it not in the streets of

64

Ashkelon, lest the daughters of the Philistines be glad. . . .

"Saul and Jonathan—in life they were loved and gracious, and in death they were not parted. They were swifter than eagles, they were stronger than lions. . . .

"How the mighty have fallen in battle! Jonathan lies slain on your heights. I grieve for you, Jonathan my brother; you were very dear to me. Your love for me was wonderful, more wonderful than that of women.

"How the mighty have fallen! The weapons of war have perished!"

So David mourned for Jonathan, his friend, and for Saul, too, despite all his unkindness. No wonder God loved David and said that he was "a man after his own heart!" *

---

* 1 Samuel 13:14.

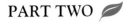

The Field of Strong Men

(2 Samuel 2:1-3:1)

NEWS of Saul's death raised big questions in David's mind. Should he proclaim himself king or wait awhile? Should he stay and rebuild Ziklag or go back and live among his own people in Judah?

As always, he took the matter to God. "Shall I go up to one of the towns of Judah?" he asked.

"Go up," God said.

"Where shall I go?"

"To Hebron."

That's how simply David talked with God, always wanting to do His will. He and his men left poor little burned-out Ziklag, "and they settled in Hebron and its towns."

It was good to be home again. Old friends were glad to see them after their long exile. In fact, the people of Judah "anointed David king over the house of Judah."

But David's troubles were not over yet. Abner, the commander in chief of Saul's army, declared that Saul's son Ish-Bosheth was the rightful heir to the throne and

66

proclaimed him king of Israel.

Now there were two kings—David, king of Judah, and Ish-Bosheth, king of Israel. Both kings had armies. Abner was the commander of one and Joab of the other.

One day these two commanders and their armies met by the pool of Gibeon. "One group sat down on one side of the pool and one group on the other side."

"Abner said to Joab, 'Let's have some of the young men get up and fight hand to hand in front of us.'

" 'All right, let them do it,' Joab said."

Twelve of the strongest young men in the ranks of David's army went out to meet 12 of the strongest young men in the ranks of Ish-Bosheth's army.

Those 24 fine young men met strength with strength and valor with valor. But they were so well matched that nobody won.

"Then each man grabbed his opponent by the head and thrust his dagger into his opponent's side, and they fell down together." All 24 died and were buried there, and the place was called "The field of swords."

Then everyone got into the fight. "The battle that day was very fierce, and Abner and the men of Israel were defeated by David's men."

Abner fled for his life, and as he was running away, he found himself being followed by Asahel, Joab's brother. He warned the young man not to come too near, but Asahel refused to listen, and Abner struck him with the butt of his spear and killed him. It was a deed that Joab never forgave.

Abner escaped, but it was the beginning of the end for him. "The war between the house of Saul and the house of David lasted a long time. David grew stronger and stronger, while the house of Saul grew weaker and weaker."

God's chosen leader was nearing the throne at last.

Two Mean Tricks

(2 Samuel 3 and 4)

AS WEEKS and months went by, Abner remained loyal to Saul's family. But after a quarrel with Ish-Bosheth, Abner decided to give his loyalty to David instead and help him become king over Israel as well as Judah.

When David heard the news he was very pleased, for he knew this would mean the end of the war. He admired Abner as a strong leader and believed that he would be as loyal to him as he once was to Saul.

He made one condition of peace—that Abner find Michal, his first wife, and bring her to him. Abner agreed at once, and sent Michal to David. Then Abner got in touch with all the elders of Israel and told them about his plan to unite the kingdom.

"For some time you have wanted to make David your king," he said. "Now do it! For the Lord promised David, 'By my servant David I will rescue my people Israel from the hand of the Philistines and from the hand of all their enemies.' "

69

When the elders of Israel had agreed to the plan, Abner told David, who invited him to dinner. "When Abner, who had twenty men with him, came to David at Hebron, David prepared a feast for him and his men."

It was a very happy time. David, big-hearted as ever, gladly overlooked all that Abner had done against him in years gone by. Abner, on the other hand, promised to do his best to bring all Israel under David's rule. "Let me go at once and assemble all Israel for my lord the king," he said, "so that they may make a compact with you, and that you may rule over all that your heart desires." David agreed and sent Abner away in peace.

That could have been the beginning of something very wonderful. But Abner never got the chance to carry out his plans. When Joab heard what had happened while he was away, he was furious.

"What have you done?" he said to David in great anger. "Look, Abner came to you. Why did you let him go? Now he is gone! You know Abner son of Ner; he came to deceive you and observe your movements and find out everything you are doing."

TWO MEAN TRICKS

To Joab, Abner was nothing more than a spy. Besides Joab hated him for killing his brother Asahel. Without telling David, he sent messengers after Abner, asking him to return to Hebron.

Supposing that David wanted to see him again, Abner gladly returned, expecting another friendly visit and perhaps another feast. But when he arrived, "Joab took him aside into the gateway, as though to speak with him privately. And there, to avenge the blood of his brother Asahel, Joab stabbed him in the stomach, and he died."

When David heard about the murder, he was horrified. He ordered Joab to put on sackcloth and mourn for the man he had killed. And when the funeral was held, "King David himself walked behind the bier."

David told his servants, "Do you not realize that a prince and a great man has fallen in Israel this day?" He was so sad and ashamed that one of his own men should have played such a mean trick that he refused to eat all day. "All the people took note and were pleased; indeed, everything the king did pleased them."

When news of Abner's death spread over the country, two

of Saul's officers, Baanah and Rechab, decided to get rid of Ish-Bosheth, the rival king. They hoped this would win David's favor.

One very hot day they came to Ish-Bosheth's house and found him lying on his bed at noon. They killed him, cut off his head, and carried the head to David. "Here is the head of Ish-Bosheth son of Saul, your enemy, who tried to take your life," they said. "This day the Lord has avenged my lord the king against Saul and his offspring."

They could not have made a greater mistake. David was even more angry with them than he had been with Joab.

"As surely as the Lord lives, who has delivered me out of all trouble," he told them, "when a man told me, 'Saul is dead,' and thought he was bringing good news, I seized him and put him to death in Ziklag. . . . How much more—when wicked men have killed an innocent man in his own house and on his own bed—should I not now demand his blood from your hand and rid the earth of you!

"So David gave an order to his men, and they killed them."

David made it clear that nothing mean or dishonest would be approved as long as he was king. 🖋

72

David Crowned King

(2 Samuel 5:1-5; 1 Chronicles 11:1-3; 11:10-12:40)

FIFTEEN years had passed since David killed Goliath. Most of this time he had spent hiding from his angry father-in-law. Now he was 30 years old, and loved by all the people from one end of the country to the other.

David had already been anointed king by the people of Judah, but now the rest of Israel, who for a while had remained loyal to Saul's son, wanted to serve him too. "When all the elders of Israel had come to King David at Hebron, . . . they anointed David king over Israel."

What a coronation that was! What a procession! The land of Palestine had never seen anything like it.

Tens of thousands of people came to the ceremony. Every tribe sent its finest troops, all fully armed. And you can be sure their swords and shields and spears were all polished until they shone like mirrors.

At the head of the long line of marching men came the soldiers of Judah—6,800 of them—all carrying shields and spears, "armed for battle." Tramp, tramp, tramp! Can't you see

them marching by?

Next came 7,100 of the tribe of Simeon, all warriors. Then 4,600 of the children of Levi, with 3,700 from the house of Aaron, including Zadok, "a brave young warrior, with 22 officers from his family."

Next in line were 3,000 men from Benjamin. Most of them had been in Saul's army till this moment.

Then came a splendid contingent—20,800 of the tribe of Ephraim, all "brave warriors, famous in their own clans."

HERBERT RUDEEN

Following these were 18,000 from the half tribe of Manasseh, each one "designated by name to come and make David king."

The tribe of Issachar sent 200 men "who understood the times and knew what Israel should do."

From Zebulun came 50,000, all marching in perfect precision. They were "experienced soldiers prepared for battle with every type of weapon" and they came "to help David with undivided loyalty."

Naphtali sent 37,000 men and 1,000 officers, all with shields and spears, and these were followed by 28,600 of the men of Dan and 40,000 from Asher.

Then from the tribes living on the other side of Jordan—Reuben, Gad, and half the tribe of Manasseh—came a mighty army numbering 120,000. What a thrilling sight that must have been!

"All these were fighting men who volunteered to serve in the ranks. They came to Hebron fully determined to make David king over all Israel. All the rest of the Israelites were also of one mind to make David king."

After the procession and the coronation there was a great feast, which lasted for three days. Of course, all those thousands of people ate a great deal of food. The Bible says that it was prepared by the tribes who lived nearest to Hebron, and they "came bringing food on donkeys, camels, mules and oxen. There were plentiful supplies of flour, fig cakes, raisin cakes, wine, oil, cattle and sheep."

Everybody was happy. "There was joy in Israel." It was a wonderful start to David's reign.

Among those present in that great throng were some of David's special friends who had stood by him through all the dark days when he was fleeing from Saul. How they must have enjoyed talking about those exciting times as they ate together!

Outstanding among them were the "three mighty men," as they were called. One of them once fought 300 men single-handed, and won. Another, in an hour of great danger, had stood shoulder to shoulder with David in a field of barley and turned the tide of battle.

Once when they were all hiding in the cave of Adullam, David had said, "Oh, that someone would get me a drink of water from the well near the gate of Bethlehem!" He longed for

76

some of that clear, cool water he had drunk so often in his boyhood days.

Then the "three mighty men" had set out to get it for him. Breaking through the ranks of the enemy, they had made their way to the well and brought back some of the water. David had been so overcome by their amazing courage and devotion that he had refused to drink the water, feeling he was unworthy of such a great sacrifice. Reverently, he had poured it out upon the ground as an offering to God.

Another famous man present at the coronation was Benaiah, who "performed great exploits" of bravery. He had killed "two of Moab's best men," and he had killed a lion in a pit on a snowy day. He once met an Egyptian giant, about seven and a half feet tall, who "had a spear like a weaver's rod." Benaiah had "snatched the spear from the Egyptian's hand and killed him with his own spear."

Together with these great heroes were other "warriors who helped him in battle." These men were armed with bows, and could use both the right hand and the left in slinging stones and shooting arrows.

Others were described as "able to handle the shield and spear. Their faces were the faces of lions, and they were as swift as gazelles in the mountains."

With such gallant men to help him, no wonder David won the war and came to the throne of Israel!

Jebus Becomes Jerusalem

(2 Samuel 5:6-25; 1 Chronicles 11:4-9; 14:1-17)

SOON after David was crowned king of Israel, he decided to take the city of Jebus from the Jebusites and make it the capital of his kingdom.

He knew the place well. It was only a few miles from Bethlehem, where he was born. When he was running away from Saul, he must have often wished that he and his men could own as fine a fortress as this.

How long the Jebusites had lived in this "fortress of Zion" nobody knows, but they were there when Israel, under Joshua, invaded Palestine. They should have been driven out then, but they weren't because the Israelites thought the place was too strong.

Having repelled many enemy attacks through the years, the Jebusites felt perfectly safe. They were sure that not even David, with all his valiant men, could take their city. They taunted him by saying that even if everybody in Jebus were blind and lame, David couldn't capture it.

But they didn't know David. They forgot that as a lad, he

78

could have been all around the city and learned its ins and outs as only a boy can. It never occurred to them that he might know that the water shaft was the one weak spot in the city's defenses—or that David himself might have climbed it when he was young.

As David planned the attack on the city, he remembered that water shaft and offered to make the first man to climb up it his commander in chief.

Joab, David's nephew, offered to lead the way. Others followed him, and the city was taken. Its name was changed to Jerusalem, and it became known as "the City of David."

Happy and proud to be in this famous fortress at last, David began putting up buildings of all kinds for his soldiers and his government. He began laying the foundations of the famous city of Jerusalem, which the people of Israel were to look upon as their beloved capital for thousands of years to come.

"And he became more and more powerful, because the Lord God Almighty was with him." Soon he became known far and wide as a wise and good ruler. Even the famous Hiram, king of Tyre, sent "cedar logs and carpenters and stonemasons" to build a house for David, which pleased him very much. Now he "knew that the Lord had established him as king over Israel."

The only people who were not pleased were Israel's old enemies, the Philistines. They felt David was becoming too strong, so they decided to fight Israel again. They "spread out in the Valley of Rephaim."

David wondered what he should do. Then, as he had often done, he turned to God for advice. "Shall I go and attack the Philistines?" he asked. "Will you hand them over to me?"

"Go," God said, "for I will surely hand the Philistines over to you."

Encouraged, David attacked them and won a great victory. They ran so quickly that they "abandoned their idols," and David and his men burned them. The sight of those idols lying on the battlefield must have reminded them of the time when Dagon fell down before the ark of the Lord.

But the Philistines did not accept defeat for long. Soon they launched another attack, and once more David asked God what he should do.

This time God told him exactly how to order the battle. He was not to make an open attack. Instead, God told him to ambush the enemy from a clump of balsam trees.

"As soon as you hear the sound of marching in the tops of the balsam trees," God said, "move quickly, because that will mean the Lord has gone out in front of you to strike the Philistine army."

David obeyed exactly. He took his men into the cluster of balsam trees and hid there, waiting for the promised sign. How they must have watched the slender tops of those balsam trees! For a long time there was not a sign of movement. The tree tops were absolutely still. Some of the men may have wondered whether there was going to be any sign at all.

Then, suddenly, it came. Just a slight fluttering at first, as gentle as if brushed by the wings of angels. More and more they tossed until the tops of the trees were waving madly in the breeze.

With a cheer the men rose from their hiding place and ran to the attack, driving the astonished Philistines in front of them in headlong flight.

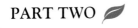

The Ark Comes Home

(2 Samuel 6:1-19; 1 Chronicles 13; 15:1-28; 16:1-36)

NOT LONG after David was crowned king of Israel, he talked with the leaders of the nation about something that had been bothering him for some time—the safety of the ark of God.

During all the troubled years of fighting between Israel and the Philistines, and between Saul and David, this sacred chest containing the Ten Commandments had been almost forgotten. It certainly was not the center of worship as it had been in the desert.

After Eli's wicked sons, Hophni and Phinehas, had taken the ark from the tabernacle, it had been captured by the Philistines. Then, after causing them plenty of trouble, it had been returned to Israel on a cart drawn by two cows. But it did not get back to the tabernacle. For some years now it had been at Kiriath Jearim, seven miles (11 kilometers) from Jerusalem, in the home of a man called Abinadab.

David felt strongly that something so old and so sacred should be properly cared for in the new national capital. "Let us

82

bring the ark of our God back to us," he said, "for we did not inquire of it during the reign of Saul."

The leaders of Israel agreed. "It seemed right to all the people. So David assembled all the Israelites, . . . to bring the ark of God from Kiriath Jearim."

Abinadab must have been surprised as he saw the people gathering around his home. Thousands upon thousands came, and at last David himself arrived.

Reverently the ark was carried out of the house and placed on a new cart for the journey to Jerusalem. Uzzah and Ahio, Abinadab's two sons, were given the honor of guiding it.

As the cart began to move, the people sang for joy. The Bible says that David and all the Israelites celebrated "with all their might before God, with songs and with harps, lyres, tambourines, cymbals and trumpets."

The singing continued as the great procession made its way toward the City of David. Everybody was so happy. Bringing the ark home seemed to mark the end of all their troubles and the dawn of a new day for Israel. Then suddenly something terrible happened.

83

As the procession was passing the threshing floor of Nacon, where the road may have been extra rough, the oxen stumbled and the cart tilted. Fearing that the ark might be thrown on the road and damaged, Uzzah put out his hand to steady it—and dropped dead.

Everyone who saw it happen was shocked. Others crowded forward to see the body. The procession stopped, and as the dreadful news was passed back from one to another the singing died away.

People began to ask why Uzzah had been killed—a question that has been asked over and over again ever since then. The only answer that could be given was that Uzzah knew very well that it was not his place to touch the ark. His act of disobedience before so many people, even though well meant, had to be punished severely.

David was very upset and decided not to take the ark farther that day. So he had it carried into the home of Obed-Edom, and everybody went home.

During the next three months, Obed-Edom's home was so wonderfully blessed that people heard of it for miles around. When David learned what was taking place, he made up his mind to make one more attempt to bring the ark to Jerusalem.

David arranged another procession, but this time he told the priests and Levites who were going to move the ark to consecrate themselves and put sin out of their lives. Trouble had come the first time, David told them, because "we did

84

not inquire of him [God] about how to do it in the prescribed way." David didn't want that to happen again.

After those who carried the ark had gone six steps, David offered up sacrifices. Then, as it moved on once more, he "danced before the Lord with all his might, while he and the entire house of Israel brought up the ark of the Lord with shouts and the sound of trumpets."

Up the steep path they went, through the gate, and into the city. And nobody irreverently touched the ark this time, you can be sure. "They brought the ark of the Lord and set it in its place inside the tent that David had pitched for it."

Then the choir sang the song David had written for this great day:

"Give thanks to the Lord, call on his name; make known among the nations what he has done. Sing to him, sing praise to him; tell of all his wonderful acts. Glory in his holy name; let the hearts of those who seek the Lord rejoice. . . .

"Sing to the Lord, all the earth; proclaim his salvation day after day. Declare his glory among the nations, his marvelous deeds among all peoples. . . .

"Praise be to the Lord, the God of Israel, from everlasting to everlasting. Then all the people said 'Amen' and 'Praise the Lord.'"

The ark was home at last.

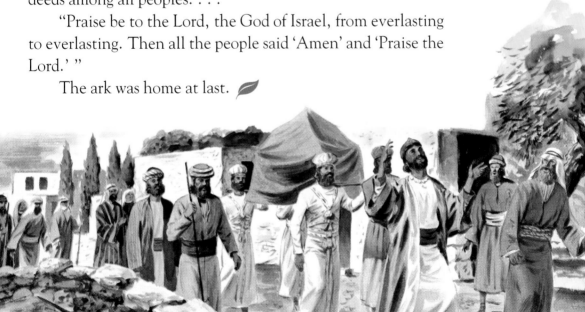

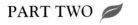

Sitting With the Lord

(2 Samuel 7:1-29; 1 Chronicles 17:1-27)

YEARS went by. David's fine new home was finished. The shepherd boy was living in a palace now, but he wasn't completely happy. Something troubled him. One day he told Nathan the prophet what was on his mind.

"Here I am," David said to him, "living in a palace of cedar, while the ark of God remains in a tent." He felt that God should have a house more beautiful than his own, even though he was the king.

Nathan was pleased that David had had such a generous thought. "Whatever you have in mind, go ahead and do it," Nathan replied to the king, "for the Lord is with you."

But that night God gave Nathan a special message for David, which the prophet passed on to him the next day. "Go and tell my servant David, 'This is what the Lord says: You are not the one to build me a house to dwell in.' "

For a moment David must have been terribly disappointed. But this was not the end of the message. "Tell my servant David, This is what the Lord Almighty says: I took you from the pasture and from following the flock to be ruler over my people Israel. I have been with you wherever you have gone, and I have cut off all your enemies from before you. Now I will make your name great, like the names of the greatest men of the earth. . . . When your days are over and you rest with your fathers, I will raise up your offspring to succeed you, . . . and I will establish his kingdom. He is the one who will build a house for my Name, and I will establish the throne of his kingdom forever. . . . Your house and your kingdom will endure forever before me; your throne will be established forever.' "

As Nathan told David what God had said about him, the king was deeply moved. At once he "went in and *sat before the Lord*," probably in the tabernacle, where he had put the ark. Here he bowed humbly before God and thanked Him for all His kindness. His prayer is one of the sweetest in all the Bible.

"Who am I, O Sovereign Lord, and what is my family, that you have brought me this far? . . . What more can David say to

you? For you know your servant, O Sovereign Lord. . . . How great you are, O Sovereign Lord! There is no one like you, and there is no God but you, . . .

"And now, Lord God, keep forever the promise you have made concerning your servant and his house. Do as you promised, so that your name will be great forever. . . .

"Now be pleased to bless the house of your servant, that it may continue forever in your sight; for you, O Sovereign Lord, have spoken, and with your blessing the house of your servant will be blessed forever."

David sat before the Lord and talked with Him as friend to friend. He did not know, of course, how God planned to fulfill His wonderful promise. He could not see the future or how through Jesus Christ his house, his name, and his kingdom would be established forever. He simply trusted God to keep His promise in His own way and in His own good time.

How lovely to talk with God like this! You can do it too. Go and sit before the Lord somewhere, just by yourself, and tell Him everything that is on your mind.

"God's Kindness"

(2 Samuel 4:4; 9:1-13)

DAVID was always doing something kind for someone else. Maybe that's another reason why God once called him a man after His own heart.

One day, as he was thinking about the past, he remembered his old friend Jonathan. He had loved Jonathan so much. What a pity he had been killed in that battle with the Philistines! If he had lived, they could have had such good times together now!

Then David wondered if any of Saul's family was still alive. He wanted to do something kind for them for Jonathan's sake. As he talked about the matter to his friends, someone suggested that a man called Ziba might know. Not only had he been a servant of Saul's, but he now had 15 sons and 20 servants, and one of them surely would be able to answer the question.

So David sent for Ziba and talked with him. "Are you Ziba?" he asked.

"Your servant," answered the man with a low bow.

"Is there no one still left of the house of Saul to whom I can

show God's kindness?"

"There is still a son of Jonathan," said Ziba. "He is crippled in both feet."

Jonathan's son still alive! It didn't seem possible.

"Where is he?" asked David eagerly.

Ziba knew exactly where he was. "He is at the house of Makir son of Ammiel in Lo Debar."

Without a moment's delay David sent messengers to Lo Debar to bring Jonathan's son, whose name was Mephibosheth.

When David saw Mephibosheth, he felt very sorry for him, because the man was lame. Mephibosheth was scared to death, too, because he was sure that the only reason for the royal summons was that David wanted to kill him. He fell on his face in front of the king, but he didn't have to be afraid.

"Mephibosheth," said David, and there was deep kindness close to love in his voice.

"Your servant," said the man.

"Don't be afraid," David said, "for I will surely show you kindness for the sake of your father Jonathan. I will restore to you all the land that belonged to your grandfather Saul, and you will always eat at my table."

Mephibosheth bowed again, hardly able to believe his ears. "What is your servant, that you should notice a dead dog like me?"

David wanted to know how Mephibosheth had become crippled. He learned that the accident had happened when Mephibosheth was 5 years old when his father Jonathan had

91

← PAINTING BY FRED COLLINS

When Mephibosheth, the lame son of Jonathan, appeared before the king he trembled with fear, but David was kind to him for Jonathan's sake, and made him a part of the royal household.

been killed. When news of Israel's defeat had reached the palace, his nurse had picked him up and fled, afraid the Philistines would surely kill Jonathan's son, too. In the wild flight to a place of safety, Mephibosheth had fallen and broken both his ankles. Since nobody had been available to set them properly, he had become lame for life.

As David listened he became still more sorry for the poor cripple and gave orders that everything possible should be done for him. Then he sent for Ziba again and said to him, "I have given your master's grandson everything that belonged to Saul and his family. You and your sons and your servants are to farm the land for him and bring in the crops, so that your master's grandson may be provided for. And Mephibosheth, grandson of your master, will always eat at my table."

Ziba said, "Your servant will do whatever my lord the king commands his servant to do."

Ziba must have been very happy, not only for what had happened to Jonathan's son but for his own good fortune, too. Caring for all Saul's land was a big job and meant plenty of work and food for his 15 sons and 20 servants.

As for Mephibosheth, he was amazed at David's goodness to him. He didn't have to live in little out-of-the-way Lo Debar anymore, but in Jerusalem. From now on he would eat "at David's table" and be treated "like one of the king's sons."

What a lovely thing David did out of love for his old friend Jonathan! This surely was "God's kindness."

92

A Rude Neighbor

(2 Samuel 10:1-19; 1 Chronicles 19:1-19)

NOT ALL of David's kind deeds were appreciated. One of them got him into a lot of trouble.

When he learned that Nabash the king of Ammon had died, he decided to send a delegation with a message of sympathy to the family. David wanted the new king, Hanun, to know that he had not forgotten Nabash's kindness when he was hiding from Saul.

But when David's messengers arrived in Ammon, they were treated as spies, not friends. The nobles of Ammon told Hanun, "Do you think David is honoring your father by sending men to you to express sympathy? Hasn't David sent them to you to explore the city and spy it out and overthrow it?"

How suspicious they were! They could not believe that a foreign king could think of doing anything so kind and gracious as to send messengers so far just to express sorrow over an old friend's death.

Young Hanun took the advice of his nobles and decided to

treat David's messengers as enemies. By his order, his men "shaved off half of each man's beard, cut off their garments in the middle . . . , and sent them away."

Imagine how ashamed and upset those poor men felt when they returned home! As for David, when he heard what had been done to his messengers, he was very angry. He told them to stay at Jericho until their beards had grown before returning to Jerusalem.

Hanun, hearing about David's anger, decided that he had better go to war with Israel before Israel went to war with him. So he sent 37 tons (34 metric tonnes) of silver to Mesopotamia and Aram, and hired 32,000 chariots and charioteers. "The Ammonites were mustered from their towns and moved out for battle."

"On hearing this, David sent Joab out with the entire army of fighting men" to meet them.

Joab, with his long experience as a general, looked over the armies lined up against him and drew up his battle plans. He decided to take the best of his men and lead them himself against the Arameans. He left the rest of the men to attack the Ammonites under the command of his brother Abishai.

Joab told Abishai, "If the Arameans are too strong for me,

94

then you are to come to my rescue; but if the Ammonites are too strong for you, then I will come to rescue you."

Then he gave this message to all his soldiers, "Be strong and let us fight bravely for our people and the cities of our God. The Lord will do what is good in his sight."

As the men of Israel went out to fight that day these challenging words kept ringing in their ears. Every soldier seemed to hear Joab saying to him, "Be strong and let us fight bravely!"

No wonder the Arameans fled!

"When the Ammonites saw that the Arameans were fleeing, they too fled before his brother Abishai" until they reached the safety of their fortress of Rabbah.

The Ammonites lost the battle and their silver as well as the friendship of Israel, all because they had treated David's delegation so rudely.

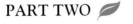

A Shadow Falls

(2 Samuel 11:1-27)

THE STORY of the defeat of the Ammonites has a sad ending. Early the following year David sent Joab with all the men of Israel to attack the Ammonite capital city, Rabbah. He knew that Israel could never feel safe again until it was taken.

Instead of going to battle with his army as he usually did, David stayed home with his family. And that's when a dark shadow fell over Jerusalem and its king.

Up to now David had been known everywhere as a good and noble man. People thought of him as a champion of right and truth. They were glad that at last there was a man on the throne who was loyal to the God of heaven. They loved him for what he had done to revive the holy religion of their fathers and for honoring God's law by bringing back the ark.

Because of David's kind and generous heart and his loyalty to God, God had richly blessed him. Through many threats and dangers, God had brought David from the sheepfold to the throne, from poverty to plenty, and had given him houses and lands and much gold and silver.

David was king over all the land from Egypt to the Euphrates. This was a fulfillment of God's promise to Abraham, "To your descendants I give this land, from the river of Egypt to the great river, the Euphrates." *

As was the custom in those days, David had many wives and lots of children. His house must have been overrun with boys and girls who called him Father. He certainly had enough to keep him happy. But he wasn't satisfied. Even though God had given him so much, he wanted more—someone he very well knew that he should not have.

Nobody likes to tell the story, but it must be told. While the army was away at Rabbah, David fell in love with the wife of Uriah the Hittite, one of his finest and noblest soldiers. Then, to make matters worse, he wrote a letter to Joab, ordering him to "put Uriah in the front line where the fighting is fiercest" so that he would be killed. And he asked Uriah to carry the letter—his own death warrant!

That shows how one mean thing leads to another.

Imagine what Joab must have thought when he received such a letter from the king! He must have wondered what had gone wrong. But he obeyed his master. Uriah was sent up close to the wall of Rabbah where "the strongest defenders were," and he died in the fighting.

When David heard the news, he thought his little plot had succeeded very well. He was sure nobody would ever find out what he had done. He waited until Uriah's wife, Bathsheba, finished mourning for her husband and then married her. What could have been more proper?

But if David thought that God did not know what he had done or did not care, he was badly mistaken. God knew all about it and was deeply disappointed. The Bible says that "the thing David had done displeased the Lord."

It was a terrible letdown. If any ordinary man had done such a thing, it would have been bad enough. But it was much worse for the king to do something like that. He should have been an example to his people. After all that David had said about keeping the Ten Commandments, he had broken them all himself! And his sinful deed had "made the enemies of the Lord show utter contempt." Even God's enemies knew how to act better than that.

So the shadow of a great sin fell over David, his family, Jerusalem, and all Israel.

---

* Genesis 15:18.

David's Repentance

(2 Samuel 12:1-13)

FOR A while David tried to live as though he had done nothing wrong. After all, he told himself, Uriah had died in battle, hadn't he? Wasn't it perfectly all right for somebody else to marry the poor man's widow? Anyway, nobody knew the truth. Joab might be suspicious, but he had no proof.

David's conscience bothered him. It gave him no rest, night or day. Then one day Nathan the prophet came to see him, and told him a story.

"There were two men in a certain town," he said, "one rich and the other poor. The rich man had a very large number of sheep and cattle, but the poor man had nothing except one little ewe lamb he had bought. He raised it, and it grew up with him and his children. . . .

"Now a traveler came to the rich man, but the rich man refrained from taking one of his own sheep or cattle to prepare a meal for the traveler who had come to him. Instead, he took the ewe lamb that belonged to the poor man and prepared it for the one who had come to him."

As David listened he became very angry. The rich man's injustice shocked him.

"As surely as the Lord lives," he exploded, "the man who did this deserves to die! He must pay for that lamb four times over, because he did such a thing and had no pity."

Suddenly the prophet, pointing at the king, cried, "You are the man!"

David turned pale. His secret was known!

Nathan went on. "This is what the Lord, the God of Israel, says: 'I anointed you king over Israel, and I delivered you from the hand of Saul. I gave your master's house to you, and your master's wives into your arms. I gave you the house of Israel and Judah. And if all this had been too little, I would have given you even more.

"Why did you despise the word of the Lord by doing what is evil in his eyes? You struck down Uriah the Hittite with the sword and took his wife to be your own. You killed him with the sword of the Ammonites."

So God knew all about it! Every horrible detail! What would his punishment be?

"This is what the Lord says," Nathan went on. " 'Out of your own household I am going to bring calamity upon you. Before your very eyes I will take your wives and give them to one who is close to you. . . . You did it in secret, but I will do this thing in broad daylight before all Israel.' "

David was crushed. In great grief he cried, "I have sinned against the Lord."

Suddenly he saw how very, very wicked he had been, how great a sin he had committed. Falling on his knees, he cried with tears, "Have mercy on me, O God, according to your unfailing love; according to your great compassion blot out my transgressions. Wash away all my iniquity and cleanse me from my sin. For I know my transgressions, and my sin is always before me. Against you, you only, have I sinned and done what is evil in your sight, . . .

"Cleanse me with hyssop, and I will be clean; wash me, and I will be whiter than snow. . . . Hide your face from my sins and blot out all my iniquity. Create in me a pure heart, O God, and renew a steadfast spirit within me. Do not cast me from your presence or take your Holy Spirit from me. Restore to me the joy of your salvation and grant me a willing spirit. . . .

"The sacrifices of God are a broken spirit; a broken and contrite heart, O God, you will not despise." [1]

God heard David's prayer. As great as his sin was, He forgave him. Right then and there He said through Nathan, "The Lord has taken away your sin. You are not going to die."

101

How kind and patient the Lord is with those who ask Him to forgive them! However great the wrong we may have done, if we are really sorry and tell Him so, He will put it behind His back. The Bible says, "If we confess our sins, he is faithful and just and will forgive us our sins and purify us from all unrighteousness." [2]

But even though God forgave David for that evil thing he did, He could not stop the consequences of it—to David, his family, and his kingdom.

That sin was the dividing point in his life. Before David sinned, he seemed to be getting stronger and stronger. After he sinned, he became weaker and weaker. Things were never the same again. He lost the respect of many of his people and of his own children. He was afraid to rebuke them for wrongdoing for fear they would say, "What about you?"

That is what sin does. It weakens. It divides. It spoils everything it touches. It takes the joy and the beauty out of life.

How true it is that the bird with the broken wing never flies so high again.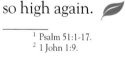

---

[1] Psalm 51:1-17.
[2] 1 John 1:9.

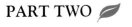

A Very Bad Son

(2 Samuel 13:23-15:30)

ONE OF David's many sons stood out above all the others. He was so good-looking and had such winning ways. His name was Absalom, and the Bible says that "in all Israel there was not a man so highly praised for his handsome appearance as Absalom. From the top of his head to the sole of his foot there was no blemish in him."

But his beauty was all on the outside. In his heart, which nobody could see, were pride, envy, hatred, and many other unlovely things.

Once he invited all of his brothers to a picnic at sheep-shearing time. All of them went, but they did not all return. When the boys got back to Jerusalem that night, two were missing. Amnon was dead, and Absalom, who had killed him, had fled, afraid of his father's anger.

Absalom stayed away from home for three long years. Finally Joab pleaded with David to allow him to come back, and David agreed.

When Absalom came home at last, he should have shown

some sign of gratitude to Joab. But he didn't. Instead, when Joab did not come to see him when Absalom thought he should, Absalom burned one of Joab's fields of barley out of spite.

It was five years after the murder of Amnon before Absalom saw his father again. That must have been a touching meeting. David forgave him for the great wrong he had done, and kissed him.

Was Absalom grateful that his life had been spared? Not at all. Instead, he began to plan a rebellion that would put him on the throne.

As a first step, he "provided himself with a chariot and horses and with fifty men to run ahead of him" so people would know how important he was. Then he began to go early every day to the main gate of the city, where he talked kindly to all the important people who came in and out.

He would ask them how far they had come and what they planned to do in Jerusalem. If a man said he had a case he wished to take to the king for judgment, Absalom would say, "Your claims are valid and proper, but there is no representative of the king to hear you. . . . If only I were appointed judge in the land! Then everyone who has a complaint or case could come to me and I would see that he gets justice."

Absalom wanted everyone to think that he would make a better king than his father. When a man bowed to him, Absalom would put his arms around him and kiss him. People began

104

talking about how kind and sympathetic a leader he was. "So he stole the hearts of the men of Israel."

When Absalom thought he had stolen enough hearts to gain the kingdom, he sent messengers secretly through all the land of Israel saying, " 'As soon as you hear the sound of the trumpets, then say, "Absalom is king in Hebron." ' . . . And so the conspiracy gained strength, and Absalom's following kept on increasing."

How many went to Hebron when Absalom set himself up

as king, we are not told. It must have been a very large number, because when a messenger arrived with the news of the rebellion, David said to all his faithful friends in Jerusalem, "Come! We must flee, or none of us will escape from Absalom. We must leave immediately, or he will move quickly to overtake us . . . and put the city to the sword."

The last thing David wanted was to have his beloved Jerusalem turned into a battlefield. With a heavy heart he decided to leave the city.

What a sad, sad day that was! The Bible says that everybody was in tears. "The whole countryside wept aloud." As for David, he "continued up the Mount of Olives, weeping as he went; his head was covered and he was barefoot. All the people with him covered their heads too and were weeping as they went up."

David, who had spent so much of his life running from his father-in-law, now was running in fear and sorrow from one of his own sons.

Caught

(2 Samuel 1:

O   N
       fi
articles of
and roaste
and chees
For they s
thirsty in

Refre
Mahanair
he had sev
and was r

At la
marching
with the
thing to :
against th
in spite o

Two Boys in a Well

(2 Samuel 15:24-27; 16:15-17:22)

I N THE time of his great sorrow David discovered who his real friends were. Crowds of people poured out of the gates of Jerusalem—men and women, boys and girls—all running from Absalom. The weeping king noticed that the chief priests, Abiathar and Zadok, were among them, bearing the ark of God. Their sons Jonathan and Ahimaaz were there, too. David stopped and spoke to them.

"Take the ark of God back into the city," he told them. "If I find favor in the Lord's eyes, he will bring me back and let me see it and his dwelling place again." Then he made his way to the desert.

Meanwhile, Absalom entered Jerusalem with his army and took over his father's palace. Calling his wisest men, he asked what he should do next. One of them, Ahithophel, advised Absalom to go after David right away and capture him. But Hushai the Archite, David's old friend, tried to delay things.

Anxious to give David time to escape, Hushai advised Absalom to wait until he could get all the men of Israel together

David wanted to lead his men into battle as he had done in the past, but they refused to let him. "You are worth ten thousand of us," they said. "It would be better now for you to give us support from the city." So David stayed behind, sitting at the city gate waiting impatiently for news.

Absalom's army did not stand a chance against David's seasoned warriors. It was soon scattered and destroyed. Fleeing on a mule, Absalom met with a strange accident. As he was passing under a great oak in the forest of Ephraim, his head caught in the branches of the tree. His mule dashed away from under him, leaving him dangling helplessly in the air.

One of David's men found Absalom in the tree and ran to tell Joab. Nothing could have pleased Joab more. He had many grievances to settle with this young man. Forgetting David's request to "be gentle" with him, Joab thrust three javelins through Absalom's heart. Then he had Absalom's body thrown into a deep pit and covered with stones.

Meanwhile, back at the city gate, David was still waiting for news. At last the watchman on the wall above him called out, "I see a man running alone."

"If he is alone," said the king, "he must have good news."

To David's surprise, the watchman cried, "I see another man running alone."

"He must be bringing good news, too," said the king, hardly able to wait for one of the messengers to arrive.

As the first runner came nearer and nearer, the watchman

110

Caught in a Tree

(2 Samuel 17:27-18:33)

ON THE other side of Jordan David found many more friends who were sorry for him and wanted to help.

One group "brought bedding and bowls and articles of pottery. They also brought wheat and barley, flour and roasted grain, beans and lentils, honey and curds, sheep, and cheese from cows' milk for David and his people to eat. For they said, 'The people have become hungry and tired and thirsty in the desert.' "

Refreshed, David and his followers went on to the city of Mahanaim. More and more men came to join his army. Soon he had several thousand of the finest soldiers in Israel with him and was ready to meet Absalom when he came to attack him.

At last the day of battle came. As the men of war were marching out of the city gate, David said to them, "Be gentle with the young man Absalom for my sake." It was a strange thing to say to an army, marching out to defend their king against the usurper to his throne. But David still loved his son, in spite of all the evil he had done.

David wanted to lead his men into battle as he had done in the past, but they refused to let him. "You are worth ten thousand of us," they said. "It would be better now for you to give us support from the city." So David stayed behind, sitting at the city gate waiting impatiently for news.

Absalom's army did not stand a chance against David's seasoned warriors. It was soon scattered and destroyed. Fleeing on a mule, Absalom met with a strange accident. As he was passing under a great oak in the forest of Ephraim, his head caught in the branches of the tree. His mule dashed away from under him, leaving him dangling helplessly in the air.

One of David's men found Absalom in the tree and ran to tell Joab. Nothing could have pleased Joab more. He had many grievances to settle with this young man. Forgetting David's request to "be gentle" with him, Joab thrust three javelins through Absalom's heart. Then he had Absalom's body thrown into a deep pit and covered with stones.

Meanwhile, back at the city gate, David was still waiting for news. At last the watchman on the wall above him called out, "I see a man running alone."

"If he is alone," said the king, "he must have good news."

To David's surprise, the watchman cried, "I see another man running alone."

"He must be bringing good news, too," said the king, hardly able to wait for one of the messengers to arrive.

As the first runner came nearer and nearer, the watchman

110

called from the wall, "It seems to me that the first one runs like Ahimaaz son of Zadok"—one of the boys who hid in the well!

"He's a good man," the king said. "He comes with good news."

As Ahimaaz reached the king he panted, "All is well," and fell down, exhausted.

"Is the young man Absalom safe?" asked David eagerly.

"I saw great confusion just as Joab was about to send the king's servant and me, your servant, but I don't know what it was," said the young man, afraid to tell the king the truth.

"Stand aside and wait here," said David, as the second runner arrived.

"My lord the king, hear the good news!" cried the Cushite. "The Lord has delivered you today from all who rose up against you."

"Is the young man Absalom safe?" asked David anxiously.

"May the enemies of my lord the king and all who rise up to harm you be like that young man," the Cushite told him.

David guessed what had happened and was heartbroken. He had hoped for victory, of course, but not at so great a price. Bursting into tears, he went up to the room over the city gate crying, "O my son Absalom! My son, my son Absalom! If only I had died instead of you—O Absalom, my son, my son!"

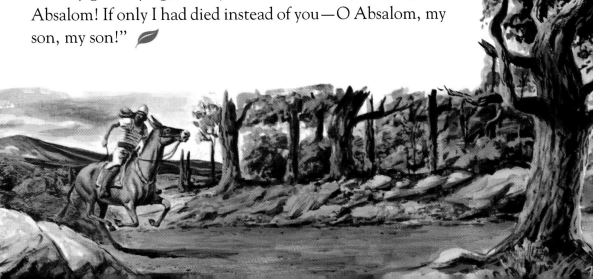

Angel Over Jerusalem

(2 Samuel 19:24-30; 22:2-33; 24:1-25; 1 Chronicles 21:1-27)

DAVID waited in Mahanaim until the trouble over Absalom had died down. Then, using the ford again, he and his men crossed the Jordan once more and climbed up the steep mountain trail to Jerusalem.

As they neared the city, Mephibosheth, Jonathan's crippled son, came to meet David. He was unkempt, because "he had not taken care of his feet or trimmed his mustache or washed his clothes from the day the king left until the day he returned safely." He explained that it was only his lameness that had kept him from going with David when he fled from Jerusalem.

At last David and his people reached the "fortress of Zion." David was so happy to be back home again that he composed this beautiful psalm:

"The Lord is my rock, my fortress and my deliverer; my God is my rock, in whom I take refuge, my shield and the horn of my salvation. He is my stronghold, my refuge and my savior. . . .

4-8

Delivered now from Saul and all his enemies, David sang: "The Lord is my rock and my fortress, and my deliverer; the God of my rock . . . my high tower, and my refuge, my saviour."

"You are my lamp, O Lord; the Lord turns my darkness into light. . . .

"For who is God besides the Lord? And who is the Rock except our God? It is God who arms me with strength and makes my way perfect."

Now that David was back on his throne, he tried to think of ways to make himself strong. Forgetting that it was God who armed him with strength, he decided to follow the example of the heathen nations around him by building up a big military force.

With this in mind he said to Joab, "Go and count the Israelites. . . . Then report back to me so that I may know how many there are."

Even Joab, hardened soldier though he was, believed David was making a mistake.

"May the Lord multiply his troops a hundred times over," he said. "My lord the king, are they not all my lord's subjects? Why does my lord want to do this? Why should he bring guilt on Israel?"

But David was obstinate. He insisted that the numbering be done. So Joab did as he was told. Some time later he came back with the figures. In all Israel and Judah, he said, there were 1,100,000 men "who could handle a sword."

Joab had scarcely left the room when David realized what he had done. Turning to God, he said, "I have sinned greatly by doing this. Now, I beg you, take away the guilt of your servant. I have done a very foolish thing."

Soon a prophet named Gad came to David and told him

114

that there was a price to pay for his sin, but he could choose his own punishment. It could be three *years* of famine, three *months* of invasion by a foreign foe, or three *days* of plague, "with the angel of the Lord ravaging every part of Israel."

It was a hard decision to make, but finally David said, "Let me fall into the hands of the Lord, for his mercy is very great; but do not let me fall into the hands of men."

A great plague fell on Israel, and many people died. The number of men Joab had counted was reduced by 70,000.

In the middle of the plague David saw a dreadful vision of the angel of the Lord over Jerusalem, his beloved city. The angel was standing "between earth and heaven" by the threshing floor of Araunah the Jebusite, and he had "a drawn sword in his hand extended over Jerusalem."

"Then David and the elders, clothed in sackcloth, fell face-down." Pleading with God to spare the people of Jerusalem, David took all the blame, crying,

"Was it not I who ordered the fighting men to be counted? I am the one who has sinned and done wrong. These are but sheep. What have they done? O Lord my God, let your hand fall upon me and my family, but do not let this plague remain on your people."

At once God sent a message through the prophet Gad, telling David to go to the threshing floor of Araunah and build an altar there. He went.

Araunah had been threshing wheat, but when he and his four sons had seen the angel, they had hidden themselves. Still trembling, they came out to meet the worried, sad-faced king.

When David asked if he could buy the place so he could build an altar there, Araunah generously replied, "Take it! . . . Look, I will give the oxen for the burnt offerings, the threshing sledges for the wood, and the wheat for the grain offering. I will give all this."

"No," David said, "I insist on paying the full price. I will not take for the Lord what is yours, or sacrifice a burnt offering that costs me nothing." David paid Araunah 15 pounds (7 kilograms) of gold for everything. Then he built an altar and laid a sacrifice on it.

Suddenly there was a flash of fire from heaven, and the sacrifice was consumed in flame and smoke. David knew then that God had forgiven him again.

The angel with the sword went back to heaven, and the plague ended.

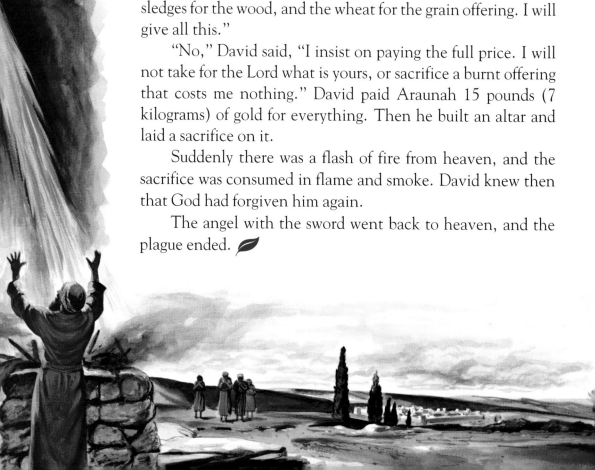

PART THREE

Stories of

Solomon

(1 Kings 1:1-11-11:43)

Henry Anderson

The Interrupted Party

(1 Kings 1:5-49; 1 Chronicles 22:2-5)

DAVID was getting to be quite an old man now, almost 70 years of age. Although his mind was still keen, he was beginning to feel the effects of his long, hard life.

He no longer led his men into battle as he had done in the past; he couldn't take the long marches over the mountains that had once been so easy.

More and more he had to stay around home. Then he had to stay in bed. But he wasn't finished yet.

There was one thing more he wanted to do. He was truly sorry for all his sins, and he yearned to do one last service for God. His plan was to build a beautiful temple, a place where the precious ark would be safe and God could be worshiped. He knew he could never finish such a temple in what was left of his lifetime, and God had told him that his son would be the one to build it. But at least he could start it.

So he gave orders that masons should start hewing great stones "for building the temple of God." He also "provided a

119

large amount of iron to make nails for the doors of the gateways and for the fittings, and more bronze than could be weighed. He also provided more cedar logs than could be counted."

Week by week and month by month the supplies poured in. As reports of the growing piles of stone, lumber, bronze, and iron reached the aging king, his old heart was filled with joy. How he wished he could live a few more years and build the Temple himself! But he knew that his son Solomon would have to carry on where he left off.

"My son Solomon is young and inexperienced," he said to himself, "and the house to be built for the Lord should be of great magnificence and fame and splendor in the sight of all the nations. Therefore I will make preparations for it."

"So David made extensive preparations before his death." But not everybody knew that it was his plan to have Solomon reign after him. Among his many sons there was a good deal of talk about which of them should wear the royal crown when father was dead. One of them, Adonijah, made up his mind that the throne should be his. "I will be king," he told himself and—just as Absalom had done years before—"he got chariots and horses ready, with fifty men to run ahead of him."

Being a fine-looking person, he made quite an impression on some people. Even Joab, general of the army, and Abiathar, the old high priest, decided that he was the one to succeed David.

Encouraged by such strong support, Adonijah made a great

120

feast and called his brothers and many of the king's servants to sit with him and hear him proclaimed king.

David, of course, knew nothing of all this. He was in bed, dreaming of the temple he wanted to build.

Suddenly Bathsheba, the mother of Solomon, burst into his room, very much upset. "My lord," she cried, "you yourself swore to me your servant by the Lord your God: 'Solomon your son shall be king after me, and he will sit on my throne.' But now Adonijah has become king, and you, my lord the king, do not know about it. He has sacrificed great numbers of cattle, fattened calves, and sheep, and has invited all the king's sons, Abiathar the priest and Joab the commander of the army, but he has not invited Solomon your servant. My lord the king, the eyes of all Israel are on you, to learn from you who will sit on the throne of my lord the king after him."

The sick, weary king stirred on his bed. The old light came back into his eyes. Nobody was going to do this to him! But

121

before he could speak, in came Nathan the prophet.

He told the same story as Bathsheba had, and asked, "Have you, my lord the king, declared that Adonijah shall be king after you, and that he will sit on your throne?"

Quickly the old king made his decision. "Call in Bathsheba," he said, and she came near him. "As surely as the Lord lives, who has delivered me out of every trouble," he said to her, "I will surely carry out today what I swore to you by the Lord, the God of Israel: Solomon your son shall be king after me, and he will sit on my throne in my place."

Next he called Zadok the priest and Nathan the prophet, and told them to anoint Solomon king of Israel, then put him on the royal mule and lead him through Jerusalem crying, "Long live King Solomon!"

These men did as they were told, and when the people saw the young man riding on David's mule, they guessed what had happened and shouted aloud in their happiness. The Bible says they rejoiced so greatly that "the ground shook with the sound" as they cried out again and again, "Long live King Solomon!"

Meanwhile, Adonijah and his friends were just finishing

their feast. As the guests were sitting around talking about what they should do next, they heard the commotion in Jerusalem. They wondered what it could mean. Joab, the old warrior, was worried most. "What's the meaning of all the noise in the city?" he asked anxiously.

He soon found out. Just then Jonathan, son of Abiathar the high priest, came running with the big news that David had abdicated in favor of Solomon.

"Zadok the priest and Nathan the prophet have anointed him king at Gihon," he gasped. "From there they have gone up cheering, and the city resounds with it. That's the noise you hear. Moreover, Solomon has taken his seat on the royal throne."

Suddenly the party was forgotten. Quickly the guests disappeared, running for their lives, afraid Solomon's friends would find them.

123

David's Glorious Farewell

(1 Chronicles 28:1-29:20)

WHEN David felt that his end was near, he wanted to speak to the leaders of Israel once more, as he had so many times in the past. He sent messengers all over the country to call together "all the officials of Israel to assemble at Jerusalem: . . . the commanders of the divisions . . . the commanders of thousands and commanders of hundreds, and the officials in charge of all the property and livestock belonging to the king and his sons, together with the palace officials, the mighty men and all the brave warriors."

Many of these leaders were his old friends. Some of the "mighty men" and the "brave warriors" had stood by him through the dark days when he was running from King Saul. They had grown old together, and now the day of parting was drawing near. Anxiously they hurried toward Jerusalem, wondering what they would find when they arrived.

They all knew that David had been bedridden for some time and that he was growing weaker every passing month.

124

They anxiously wondered if this would be the very last time they would see him.

One by one they filed into the crowded meeting place, their faces grave and worried. Soon David was brought in, perhaps on a couch or bed. How good it was to see him again! Yet how sad that their once mighty leader was now so old and feeble!

But there was no accounting for David. He seemed to have secret reserves of strength for every emergency. Again and again through his long, danger-filled life, he had surprised both friends and enemies in times when they thought he had been defeated. Now it happened again. Suddenly the old king rallied. Rising to his feet, he began to speak with much of the power and authority of other days.

"Listen to me, my brothers and my people," said the grand old man. "I had it in my heart to build a house as a place of rest for the ark of the covenant of the Lord, for the footstool of our God, and I made plans to build it. But God said to me, 'You are not to build a house for my Name, because you are a warrior and have shed blood.' . . .

"Of all my sons—and the Lord has given me many—he has

125

chosen my son Solomon to sit on the throne of the kingdom of the Lord over Israel.

"He said to me: 'Solomon your son is the one who will build my house and my courts, for I have chosen him to be my son, and I will be his father. I will establish his kingdom forever if he is unswerving in carrying out my commands and laws, as is being done at this time.'

"So now I charge you in the sight of all Israel and of the assembly of the Lord, and in the hearing of our God: Be careful to follow all the commands of the Lord your God, that you may possess this good land and pass it on as an inheritance to your descendants forever."

Turning to his son Solomon who was close beside him, he said, "And you, my son Solomon, acknowledge the God of your father, and serve him with wholehearted devotion and with a willing mind, for the Lord searches every heart and understands every motive behind the thoughts. If you seek him, he will be found by you; but if you forsake him, he will reject you forever.

"Consider now, for the Lord has chosen you to build a temple as a sanctuary. Be strong and do the work."

Then David gave his son the blueprints he had prepared for every detail of the great and beautiful building he had planned. Included were "the plans for the portico of the Temple, its buildings, its storerooms, its upper parts, its inner rooms and the place of atonement," and much, much more.

" 'All this,' David said, 'I have in writing from the hand of the Lord upon me, and he gave me understanding in all the details of the plan.' "

Everybody must have been astonished at these words. Few of those present could have had any idea that all the plans were ready for the new Temple or that God had described them personally to the king. This was just like what had happened centuries before on Mount Sinai, when God showed Moses the pattern of the desert tabernacle!

Turning to the congregation again, David told them about all the other preparations he had made for the building, including the stores of gold, silver, bronze, iron, wood, and precious stones he had gathered together.

Then he told them what his own personal gift would be— the last gift he would ever be able to make to God. "I now give my personal treasures of gold and silver for the temple of my God, over and above everything I have provided for this holy temple: three thousand talents of gold . . . and seven thousand talents of refined silver."

Everyone listening was deeply touched. What a magnificent gift this was from their beloved leader, old, weak, and dying though he was! It was hard for some to keep from weeping.

127

A moment later something wonderful began to happen. One by one the leaders of Israel came forward with their own rich gifts and pledges of gold, silver, bronze, iron, and precious stones.

Nothing like this had happened since that day in the desert when the people had brought their treasures to Moses to build the tabernacle. It seemed as though everybody present wanted to have some part in helping to make the old king's dream come true. Gladly they brought him the best they had, rejoicing at the look of gratitude and happiness on his dear old face.

"The people rejoiced at the willing response of their leaders, for they had given freely and wholeheartedly to the Lord. David the king also rejoiced greatly."

When the last of the people had presented their offerings, David praised the Lord before the whole congregation. Using some of the most beautiful words in all the Bible, he said:

"Praise be to you, O Lord, God of our father Israel, from everlasting to everlasting. Yours, O Lord, is the greatness and the power and the glory and the majesty and the splendor, for everything in heaven and earth is yours. Yours, O Lord, is the kingdom; you are exalted as head over all. Wealth and honor come from you; you are the ruler of all things. . . . Now, our God, we give you thanks, and praise your glorious name. . . .

"O Lord our God, as for all this abundance that we have provided for building you a temple for your Holy Name, it comes from your hand, and all of it belongs to you. . . . O Lord, God of our fathers Abraham, Isaac and Israel, keep this desire

128

in the hearts of your people forever, and keep their hearts loyal to you."

Then, so tenderly, he prayed for his son. "Give my son Solomon the wholehearted devotion to keep your commands, requirements and decrees and to do everything to build the palatial structure for which I have provided."

"Praise the Lord your God," he said to the assembly, and together with the old king, they bowed their heads and worshiped.

It was a noble and glorious finish to the life of a man who, in spite of his many mistakes, had tried to serve God the best he knew how.

Solomon's Prayer for Wisdom

(1 Kings 3:4-15; 1 Chronicles 29:21-25)

THE VERY next day after David had made his last speech to his people, he held a great feast in Jerusalem, and for the second time made Solomon king.

Most of the leaders of Israel had not been present when David had sent Solomon through the city on his royal mule in order to stop Adonijah's attempt to seize the throne. Now that Israel's leaders were all in the city to say goodbye to their old king, everyone gathered together for another coronation. "They acknowledged Solomon son of David as king a second time, anointing him before the Lord to be ruler. . . . So Solomon sat on the throne of the Lord as king in place of his father David. He prospered and all Israel obeyed him.

"All the officers and mighty men, as well as all of King David's sons, pledged their submission to King Solomon.

"The Lord highly exalted Solomon in the sight of all Israel and bestowed on him royal splendor such as no king over Israel ever had before."

There was a reason why God conferred high honor and

great blessing on the young man: he was so eager to do right.

Soon after his coronation Solomon called all the leaders of Israel to meet him at Gibeon where the old desert tabernacle was still standing. The ark was not there anymore, because David had moved it for safekeeping into Jerusalem. But the bronze altar made by Bezalel was still in its old place outside the faded tent, and Solomon offered a thousand burnt offerings on it as a mark of his devotion to God.

The fact that he, the new young king, was starting his reign this way must have made a great impression on everybody who was there. Quickly the story spread all over the country, bringing hope of a great revival.

One night while Solomon was in Gibeon, the Lord appeared to him in a dream and asked, " 'Ask for whatever you want me to give you.'

"Solomon answered, 'You have shown great kindness to your servant, my father David, because he was faithful to you and righteous and upright in heart. You have continued this great kindness to him and have given him a son to sit on his throne this very day.

" 'Now, O Lord my God, you have made your servant king in place of my father David. But I am only a little child and do not know how to carry out my duties. Your servant is here among the people you have chosen, a great people, too numerous to count or number.

" 'So give your servant a discerning heart to govern your

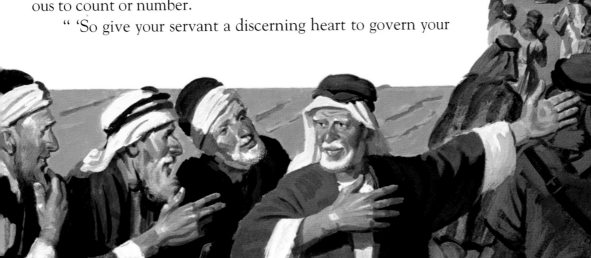

people and to distinguish between right and wrong. For who is able to govern this great people of yours?'"

God was very pleased with Solomon's prayer. What a noble petition it was! Many other young men would have asked for a nice new chariot, or a gold-plated suit of armor, or maybe some fine Arabian horses, but not this youth. He asked for wisdom to do his job as it should be done.

SOLOMON'S PRAYER FOR WISDOM

God said to him, "Since you have asked for this and not for long life or wealth for yourself, nor have asked for the death of your enemies but for discernment in administering justice, I will do what you have asked. I will give you a wise and discerning heart. . . . Moreover, I will give you what you have not asked for—both riches and honor—so that in your lifetime you will have no equal among kings. And if you walk in my ways and obey my statutes and commands as David your father did, I will give you a long life."

"Then Solomon awoke—and he realized it had been a dream."

But what a beautiful dream! And what a lesson it has for every boy and girl today!

If God asked you, "What shall I give you?" what would you say to Him? Would you ask for the latest model car? Or for a beautiful, expensive home? Or for lots of money? Or to be at the top of your class? Or to win first prize at your school games?

Or would you say, like Solomon, "Just make me wise, dear Lord, so that I may always choose what is right, and please You in everything I do"?

If you will pray a prayer like this, asking only for wisdom to do God's will, it will please Him very much indeed. And He will answer you as surely as He did King Solomon, giving you not only wisdom but everything else you need. ✐

133

← PAINTING BY HARRY ANDERSON

As newly appointed ruler of the kingdom Solomon felt his responsibility so much that he asked God not for fame or wealth or power, but only for wisdom to rule his people.

Dividing a Baby

(1 Kings 3:16-28)

ONE OF the first problems the new king met was a very difficult one. Two women came to him, both claiming the same baby. They wanted him to decide whose it was. But how could he tell? Sitting on his throne, Solomon listened carefully to their stories.

The two women lived together in the same house. Their babies had been born about the same time, one three days before the other. Then one of the babies had died.

The first woman said, "My lord. . . . During the night this woman's son died because she lay on him. So she got up in the middle of the night and took my son from my side while I your servant was asleep. She put him by her breast and put her dead son by my breast."

When she awoke in the morning to feed her baby, the first woman said, she found a dead child in her arms that was not hers but the other woman's.

"No!" cried the other woman frantically, "the living one is my son; the dead one is yours!"

134

"No!" yelled the first woman, "the dead one is yours; the living one is mine."

What a scene that must have been in the palace, with these two angry women shouting at each other, ready to tear out each other's hair if they had the chance!

Poor Solomon! He had never met anything like this before. If ever he needed the wisdom which God had promised him, it was now.

"Bring me a sword," he said calmly, and a servant brought him one, while silence fell in the room.

"Whatever is he going to do with that sword?" someone whispered.

"Now the baby!" said the king.

There was a gasp. Surely he was not going to cut the baby in half!

"Cut the living child in two," said Solomon, "and

give half to one and half to the other.''

Everybody was shocked.

''No! Please don't!'' screamed the real mother. ''Please, my lord, give her the living baby! Don't kill him.''

''No,'' said the other woman heartlessly. ''Neither I nor you shall have him. Cut him in two!''

''Aha!'' mused Solomon. ''Now I know which one is the child's mother.'' Pointing to the woman who had asked that the baby's life be spared, he said, ''Give the living baby to the first woman. Do not kill him; she is his mother.''

As the two women went out from the presence of the king their story went with them. It leaped from city to city and from village to village until everybody from one end of the country to the other was talking about that baby and how Solomon had found out who its mother was.

''When all Israel heard the verdict the king had given, they held the king in awe, because they saw that he had wisdom from God to administer justice.''

Israel's Happiest Days

(1 Kings 4:20-5:18)

UNDER King Solomon, the children of Israel enjoyed their happiest days. Never had they been so rich. Never had they known such peace.

"The people of Judah and Israel were as numerous as the sand on the seashore; they ate, they drank and they were happy." Those were good times indeed!

"And Solomon ruled over all the kingdoms from the River to the land of the Philistines, as far as the border of Egypt. These countries brought tribute and were Solomon's subjects all his life. . . . For he ruled over all the kingdoms . . . and had peace on all sides. During Solomon's lifetime Judah and Israel, from Dan to Beersheba, lived in safety, each man under his own vine and fig tree."

With no enemies to fear and no wars to fight, Solomon was able to devote himself almost entirely to the task of building the Temple his father had planned and prepared for so lovingly.

Though David had made great preparations, gathering lumber and metals of various kinds, they were not enough. As

137

Solomon looked over the plans for the Temple his father had given him, he saw that he would need much more material before he could start to build.

So he sent a message to David's old friend Hiram, king of Tyre, asking him for help. In particular, Solomon wanted more cedar and pine trees out of the forests of Lebanon and offered to send some of his men to help cut the trees. He would also pay Hiram's workers well, "for," he said graciously, "you know that we have no one so skilled in felling timber as the Sidonians."

King Hiram was equally courteous and sent back a message, saying, "Praise be to the Lord today, for he has given David a wise son to rule over this great nation." Then he promised to do everything Solomon asked.

"I . . . will do all you want in providing the cedar and pine logs," he wrote. "My men will haul them down from Lebanon to the sea, and I will float them in rafts by sea to the place you specify. . . . You can take them away."

Many more trees were felled and floated down the coast as far as Joppa. Then Solomon's men hauled them up the steep road to Jerusalem. It was a long, difficult task, and took years to complete.

"Solomon gave Hiram twenty thousand cors of wheat as food for his household, in addition to twenty thousand baths of pressed olive oil. Solomon continued to do this

for Hiram year after year."

To help Hiram in the cutting and sawing, Solomon called for 30,000 men, sending 10,000 every month to Lebanon in rotation. In addition, he had 70,000 more men helping in other ways, and 80,000 "stonecutters in the hills."

At the king's command, these men brought "large blocks of quality stone to provide a foundation of dressed stone for the temple. The craftsmen of Solomon and Hiram and the men of Gebal cut and prepared the timber and stone for the building of the temple."

What excitement there must have been as the piles of lumber and cut stones grew greater and greater! For by this time the building of the Temple had become the center of interest for all Israel. With so many thousands at work on the project, and so many more thousands busy feeding them, it must have been the main topic of conversation from one end of the country to the other.

Nobody minded the work. It was so much better than fighting the Philistines, the Amalekites, the Ammonites, and the rest of their enemies, as they had had to do for so many weary, discouraging years.

A great new day had dawned for Israel. Peace! How wonderful it was! God was blessing His people as He had promised Abraham, Isaac, and Jacob long ago. What a privilege it was to help build a Temple for the glory of His name!

Huram, the Bronze Caster

(1 Kings 7:13-46; 2 Chronicles 2:7-18; 3:15-4:17)

SOLOMON had one very special request to make of King Hiram of Tyre. He needed a man skilled in handling metals. "Send me, therefore, a man skilled to work in gold and silver, bronze and iron," he wrote to his friend.

What he needed was another Bezalel, who did such wonderful work in building the desert tabernacle and its furniture. And King Hiram found such a man. His name was Huram, a citizen of Tyre, whose mother belonged to the tribe of Dan. Strangely, he was distantly related, through his mother, to Aholiab, who had been Bezalel's right-hand helper nearly 500 years before.

This young man, just like Bezalel and Aholiab, was "highly skilled and experienced" and "trained to work in gold and silver, bronze and iron, stone and wood, and with purple and blue and crimson yarn and fine linen. He is experienced in all kinds of engraving and can execute any design given to him." A wonder worker!

140

HURAM, THE BRONZE CASTER

The king's description was not overdrawn—not when you know what young Huram did. When he arrived in Jerusalem and looked over the plans of the Temple, he saw that his biggest job was to cast two great pillars of bronze that were to stand in front of it.

These pillars were to be 27 feet high (8 meters) and almost 6 feet (2 meters) thick. Where could such massive pillars be cast? Where could enough clay be found to make the molds for them?

It was a problem that would have stumped most people, but not Huram. He looked around until he found the clay—down in the Jordan valley "between Succoth and Zarathan."

Then he must have asked himself, "Shall I take the metal to the clay or bring the clay to the metal?" Either way meant an immense amount of work.

He decided to cast the pillars in the valley. So he set up his furnaces down there, melted the metal, then poured it into the molds he had fashioned in the clay ground.

Finally, when everything was done, he produced two magnificent pillars of gleaming bronze.

But now he had to get them up the mountain to Jerusalem. How did he do it? Nobody knows for sure. The pillars were long and heavy, and the mountain trail was steep and winding, with many hairpin bends. But there was no stopping Huram. Somehow or other he got those two pillars up to Jerusalem and put them in place before the Temple.

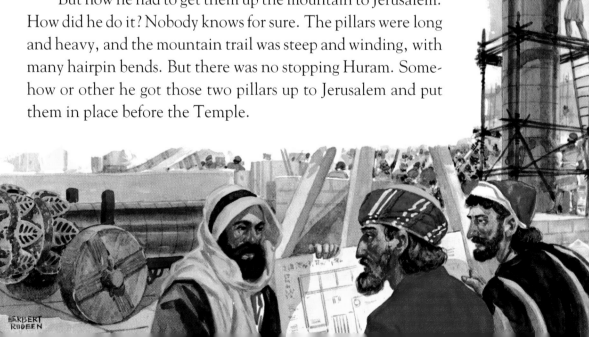

One pillar was known as "Jakin," meaning "He shall establish," and the other was called "Boaz," meaning, "In him is strength." They stood for hundreds of years to the glory of God, a reminder of what a man can do when he puts his mind to his work.

While Huram's laborers were still working on the pillars and dragging them inch by inch up the mountainside, he was busy making many other things. Some of them were almost as big and important as the two great pillars. For instance, he made a great bronze bowl, or "Sea," 15 feet (4.5 meters) in diameter and over 7 feet (2 meters) deep. This rested on 12 bronze bulls, "three facing north, three facing west, three facing south and three facing east."

This was no easy task, for the huge bowl was made of metal "a handbreadth in thickness, and its rim was like the rim of a cup, like a lily blossom. It held three thousand baths." In today's measurements, that would be almost 12,000 gallons (43,500 liters).

Some of the other things Huram made are listed in the record: "four hundred pomegranates," and "ten stands with their ten basins; . . . the pots, shovels and sprinkling bowls," all of "burnished bronze."

Huram helped build the Temple in many other ways. When we speak of that beautiful house of God as Solomon's Temple, we should not forget all the labor of love which he and thousands of other people put into it.

Building in Silence

(1 Kings 6:1-38; 2 Chronicles 3:1-4:11)

IT TOOK Solomon four years to gather all the material needed to build the Temple, and seven more years to put it together.

One reason why the preparations took so long was that every stone and every piece of metal or wood was cut to size or molded to shape before it was brought to the building site. As a result, not a sound was heard while the Temple was taking shape. "No hammer, chisel or any other iron tool was heard at the temple site while it was being built."

The Temple was built as silently as God works in nature, when He makes the grass grow and the trees bud, blossom, and bear fruit. Perhaps God intended it to be a lesson to His people to remind them how He plans to build His church on earth. Instead of using loud, noisy methods, His Holy Spirit works quietly on the hearts of men and women, boys and girls.

As stone was laid on stone, each fitting perfectly in its proper place, the building gradually took shape. Fathers and mothers from Jerusalem and nearby villages brought their children to see the great sight and gaze in wonder as the silent builders worked. For years—long before David's death—they had heard stories about the glorious Temple; now it was growing before their eyes. And from the huge size of the blocks of stone being used for the foundations, they could see it was going to be even more wonderful than they had dreamed.

The Temple was exactly twice as large as the tabernacle Moses built in the wilderness. Moses' tabernacle was 45 feet (14 meters) long, and Solomon's Temple was 90 feet (27.4 meters) long.

Moses' tabernacle was 15 feet (4.5 meters) wide, and Solomon's Temple was 30 feet (9 meters) wide.

Moses' tabernacle was 15 feet (4.5 meters) high, and Solomon's Temple was 30 feet (9 meters) high.

The desert tabernacle had been divided into two parts— the holy place and the Most Holy Place. So Solomon's Temple was arranged in the same way.

All the walls and ceiling were lined with cedar, and the floor was covered with "planks of pine. . . . No stone was to be seen." Then all the wood was covered with gold. Solomon "overlaid the ceiling beams, doorframes, walls and doors of the temple with gold, and he carved cherubim on the walls. . . . He made the curtain of blue, purple and crimson yarn and fine linen, with cherubim worked into it."

In the Most Holy Place, he put two cherubim carved from olive wood and covered with gold. The cherubim's

144

wings touched the walls on either side.

In the holy place he put a new golden altar of incense, a new golden table for the bread of the Presence, and 10 golden lampstands, five on the right side and five on the left.

How beautiful it must have been inside, with the bright colors of the curtain and the twinkling lights of the 10 lampstands, all reflected in the polished gold of the walls, floor, and ceiling!

Outside the Temple a huge bronze altar, 30 feet (9 meters) square and 15 feet (4.5 meters) high, was built for offering sacrifices.

The "Sea" Huram had made, which was really a bathing pool for the priests, stood at the southeast corner. Beside this were 10 bronze lavers, or wash places, for washing the sacrifices before they were offered.

At last, seven years after the work was started, the building was finished. The plans that God had given to David had been carried out to the letter. Everything, from the laying of the foundation stones to the polishing of the last bronze pomegranate, had been done as well as the people could do it. Everyone, from Solomon to the humblest stonecutter, had done his best to make this the most glorious temple ever built.

Now all that was left to do was the dedication. Would God accept this building as His own and honor it with His presence as He had honored the tabernacle in the desert?

The Temple Dedicated

(1 Kings 8:1-50; 2 Chronicles 5:1-8:1-61)

ONE THING was missing from the Temple.
The golden lampstands were in place, as well as
the golden tables for the bread of the Presence, the
golden altar of incense, the many-colored curtains, and the
two golden cherubim—but there was no ark. It was still in the
tent which David had made for it when he had brought it
from Kiriath Jearim to Jerusalem.

So when all the work on the Temple was done and everything had been made as perfect as possible, "Solomon sum-
moned to Jerusalem the elders of Israel, all the heads of the
tribes and the chiefs of the Israelite families, to bring up the ark
of the Lord's covenant from Zion, the City of David."

What a procession that must have been! And what joy
must have filled every heart as the people saw the precious ark,
now nearly 500 years old. The Levites carried it reverently to
what all believed would be its final resting place in the Most
Holy Place of the beautiful new Temple. At the same time the
priests and Levites brought all that was left of the old taberna-

146

cle, with "all the sacred furnishings" that were in it, and stored them carefully in the new building.

As the priests "brought the ark of the Lord's covenant to its place . . . and put it beneath the wings of the cherubim" they must have noticed how small it seemed. It was only 45 inches (1.1 meter) long and 27 inches (.7 meter) wide, while the new Most Holy Place was 30 feet (9 meters) square and 36 feet (11 meters) high, and each of the cherubim was 15 feet from wing tip to wing tip.

Yet, though the ark was so small and empty, except for "the two tablets that Moses had placed in it at Horeb," it was the most precious and important thing in the Temple. Without the ark and all that it represented, the services in the Temple would have been meaningless.

Suddenly, as the priests came out of the Temple, having left the ark in the Most Holy Place, there was a great burst of music and song. A hundred and twenty priests blew trumpets, while scores of Levites began to play on cymbals, harps, and lyres, and others started to sing the praises of God.

"The trumpeters and singers joined in unison, as with one voice, to give praise and thanks to the Lord. Accompanied by trumpets, cymbals and other instruments, they raised their voices in praise to the Lord and sang: 'He is good; his love

endures forever.' Then the temple of the Lord was filled with a cloud."

Solomon, standing on a bronze platform five feet (1.5 meters) high in front of the Temple, was told what had happened. He knew the cloud meant that "the glory of the Lord filled the temple of God." Deeply moved that God had been pleased to show this mark of approval, he "spread out his hands toward heaven" before the thousands of people crowded around him, and prayed a beautiful prayer of dedication.

"O Lord, God of Israel," he cried, "there is no God like you in heaven or on earth—you who keep your covenant of love with your servants who continue wholeheartedly in your way. . . . But will God really dwell on earth with men? The heavens, even the highest heavens, cannot contain you. How much less this temple I have built!

"Yet give attention to your servant's prayer and his plea for mercy, O Lord my God. Hear the cry and the prayer that your servant is praying in your presence. May your eyes be open toward this temple day and night, this place of which you said you would put your Name there. May you hear the prayer your servant prays toward this place.

148

"Hear the supplications of your servant and of your people Israel when they pray toward this place. Hear from heaven, your dwelling place; and when you hear, forgive."

Then the king made seven special requests of God:

1. "When a man wrongs his neighbor" and the matter is brought to the Temple, "hear from heaven, and act. Judge between your servants."

2. "When your people Israel have been defeated by an enemy because they have sinned against you and when they turn back and confess your name, praying and making supplication before you in this temple, then hear from heaven and forgive the sin of your people."

3. In time of drought, when there is no rain, "when they pray toward this place and confess your name and turn from their sin . . . , then hear from heaven and forgive the sin of your servants. . . . Send rain on the land."

4. "When famine or plague comes to the land, or blight or mildew, locusts or grasshoppers, . . . whatever disaster or disease may come, and when a prayer or plea is made by any of your people Israel—each one aware of his afflictions and pains, and spreading out his hands toward this temple—then hear from heaven, your dwelling place. Forgive."

5. If a foreigner comes from a distant land and prays in this house, "hear from heaven, your dwelling place, and do whatever the foreigner asks of you, so that all the peoples of the earth may know your name."

149

6. "When your people go to war against their enemies, wherever you send them, and when they pray to you toward this city . . . and the temple I have built for your Name, then hear from heaven their prayer and their plea, and uphold their cause."

7. "When they sin against you—for there is no one who does not sin—and you become angry with them and give them over to the enemy, who takes them captive to a land far away or near; . . . and if they turn back to you with all their heart and soul in the land of their captivity . . . , then from heaven, your dwelling place, hear their prayer. . . . And forgive."

Then, as Solomon ended his prayer, he cried, "Now arise, O Lord God, and come to your resting place, you and the ark of your might. May your priests, O Lord God, be clothed with salvation, may your saints rejoice in your goodness."

It was such a beautiful prayer! So full of kindness and

thoughtfulness for others! And there is no doubt that God heard it in heaven, His dwelling place. For no sooner had Solomon finished praying than "fire came down from heaven and consumed the burnt offering and the sacrifices, and the glory of the Lord filled the temple."

When all the thousands who had gathered for this great and glorious ceremony saw the fire fall and saw the beautiful new Temple radiant with the glory of the Lord, "they knelt on the pavement with their faces to the ground, and they worshiped and gave thanks to the Lord, saying, 'He is good; his love endures forever.' "

And when the mothers put their children to bed that night, I am sure that more than one boy or girl must have said, "Mamma, did you see the fire come down from heaven today? Wasn't it wonderful? How near God must have been just then!"

Words of Warning

(1 Kings 8:62-9:9)

AFTER the solemn service of dedication, Solomon held a great feast for all the crowds who had come to Jerusalem. It lasted 14 days. "On the following day he sent the people away. They blessed the king and then went home, joyful and glad in heart for all the good things the Lord had done for his servant David and his people Israel."

When they had all gone home and things had begun to settle down again, "the Lord appeared to him a second time."

The first time was at Gibeon, just after his coronation, when he had prayed that lovely prayer for wisdom and God had granted his request. Now the Lord had something more to say to him.

"I have heard the prayer and plea you have made before me," He said, referring to his prayer at the dedication of the Temple. "I have consecrated this temple, which you have built, by putting my Name there forever. . . . If you walk before me in integrity of heart and uprightness, as David your father did, and do all I command, . . . I will establish your royal throne over Israel forever.

"But"—and at this Solomon must have listened with some anxiety—"if you or your sons turn away from me and do not observe the commands and decrees I have given you and go off to serve other gods and worship them, then I will cut off Israel from the land I have given them and will reject this temple I have consecrated for my Name. Israel will then become a byword and an object of ridicule among all peoples. And though this temple is now imposing, all who pass by will be appalled and will scoff and say, 'Why has the Lord done such a thing to this land and to this temple?'

"People will answer, 'Because they have forsaken the Lord their God.' "

This house, this glorious Temple, rejected! *How could that ever be?* thought Solomon. Impossible! Surely God would never let anything so beautiful, so solidly built, be destroyed!

These were strange words for God to use about a building on which the young king had spent seven of the best years of his life. Did God need to give such a solemn warning?

He did, as we shall see.

Already Solomon had married the daughter of the king of

Egypt, and there was always the danger that her children might want to worship the heathen gods she once served. Already he was fast becoming the richest man in the world, with more gold and silver pouring into Jerusalem than its people had ever seen before. Already he was beginning to spend money lavishly and to live in luxury. That sort of life always endangers a person's relationship to God.

That's why God warned Solomon to be careful how he lived from now on. God wanted him to remember that obedience to His commandments is more important in His sight than all the beautiful buildings ever built.

Doing God's will, speaking the truth, thinking pure thoughts, living a godly life — these mean far more to Him than the best and biggest things any of us can build of stone, or wood, or gold, or silver.

Oh, yes, God wanted the Temple Solomon had built to stand forever. He said so. But only if Solomon and his children would be true to Him always. If they turned their backs on Him and followed other gods, then the Temple would disappear from the face of the earth. No matter how firm its foundations, how massive its walls, how costly its golden ornaments, it would be carried away like chaff before the wind.

Solomon's Temple is not to be found in Jerusalem today because God's word came true. His warning was forgotten, and the Temple was completely destroyed.

The Queen of Sheba

(1 Kings 10:1-11:6; 2 Chronicles 9:1-27)

AS NEWS of Solomon's wealth and wisdom spread abroad, more and more kings and rulers came to visit him. "All the kings of the earth sought audience with Solomon to hear the wisdom God had put in his heart. Year after year, everyone who came brought a gift—articles of silver and gold, and robes, weapons and spices, and horses and mules."

"All the kings of Arabia and the governors of the land brought gold and silver to Solomon." And as each visitor brought some rich present, Solomon grew richer and richer.

The gold that came to him in one year weighed 25 tons (23 metric tonnes)—a very large sum of money—besides what came to him from "merchants and traders."

To increase his wealth even more, he built two fleets, one on the Red Sea to bring gold from the land of Ophir, and one on the Mediterranean Sea to trade with lands to the west. "Once every three years" these ships came home, "carrying gold, silver and ivory, and apes and baboons."

HERBERT
RUDEEN

THE QUEEN OF SHEBA

He had 1,400 chariots and 1,200 horses, and he made silver as common as stones in Jerusalem. "All King Solomon's goblets were gold. . . . Nothing was made of silver, because silver was considered of little value in Solomon's days."

With some of his wealth, Solomon built "a great throne inlaid with ivory and overlaid with fine gold. The throne had 6 steps," with lions on either side of each step and 2 more on either side of the throne itself, making 14 lions in all. No wonder the Bible says, "Nothing like it had ever been made for any other kingdom." It must have made quite an impression on visitors.

Among the many famous people who came to see Solomon was the Queen of Sheba. She lived, many believe, in the southern part of Arabia. Her journey to Jerusalem was a long and tiring one, for she came "with a very great caravan—with camels carrying spices, large quantities of gold, and precious stones."

She must have been a very wise woman herself, because she was eager for more knowledge. Having heard of Solomon's famous wisdom, she "came to Jerusalem to test him with hard questions." The Bible doesn't tell us what her questions were about, but it does say that Solomon answered them all, and this made her very happy.

Perhaps she even walked up the six steps of the magnificent gold and ivory throne, between the 12 lions. In any case, when she had seen "all the wisdom of Solomon and the palace he had built, the food on his table, the seating of his officials, the attending servants in their robes, his cupbearers, and the burnt

157

ccompanied by a long column of servants, orses, and camels carrying spices, gold, pre- ious stones, and other riches of her kingdom, he Queen of Sheba came to visit Solomon.

offerings he made at the temple of the Lord, she was overwhelmed."

"The report I heard in my own country about your achievements and your wisdom is true," she said to the king. "But I did not believe these things until I came and saw with my own eyes. Indeed, not even half was told me; in wisdom and wealth you have far exceeded the report I heard. How happy your men must be! How happy your officials, who continually stand before you and hear your wisdom!"

Then she added this word of praise to Solomon's God, giving Him the glory for all that she had seen and heard: "Praise be to the Lord your God, who has delighted in you and placed you on the throne of Israel. Because of the Lord's eternal love for Israel, he has made you king, to maintain justice and righteousness."

Then she gave Solomon 4½ tons (4 metric tonnes) of gold and "large quantities of spices, and precious stones. Never again were so many spices brought in as those the queen of Sheba gave to King Solomon."

As she returned to her own country the queen took away with her the wonderful memory of a king whom the God of heaven had greatly prospered and of a land richly blessed.

If only Solomon had continued to witness for his God like this, how much good he might have done! How many kings and queens might have learned of God's goodness and love! With his wealth and wisdom, Solomon could have filled the world with the knowledge of the Lord. But he didn't. The world's wisest man was one of God's worst disappointments.

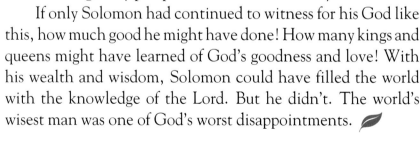

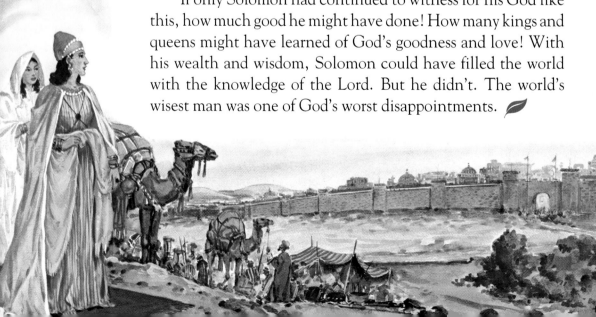

Wisdom of the Wise

(Proverbs)

D AY AFTER day, year after year, a river of wisdom flowed from Solomon's bright, keen mind. "He spoke three thousand proverbs and his songs numbered a thousand and five." *

He must have had a scribe, or secretary, to write down his wise sayings as he thought of them. Many are found in the books of Proverbs and Ecclesiastes.

Here is some of his good advice for students:

"If you call out for insight and cry aloud for understanding, and if you look for it as for silver and search for it as for hidden treasure, then you will understand the fear of the Lord and find the knowledge of God" (Proverbs 2:3-5).

Every boy and girl should memorize this and the above verse: "Trust in the Lord with all your heart and lean not on your own understanding; in all your ways acknowledge him, and he will make your paths straight" (Proverbs 3:5).

Here is more good counsel for young and old: "Do not set foot on the path of the wicked or walk in the way of evil men.

Avoid it, do not travel on it; turn from it and go on your way. . . . The path of the righteous is like the first gleam of dawn, shining ever brighter till the full light of day" (Proverbs 4:14-18).

Watching some ants one day, he saw a lesson for lazy people: "Go to the ant, you sluggard; consider its ways and be wise! It has no commander, no overseer or ruler, yet it stores its provisions in summer and gathers its food at harvest. . . . A little sleep, a little slumber, a little folding of the hands to rest—and poverty will come on you like a bandit and scarcity like an armed man" (Proverbs 6:6-11).

He had some very wise things to say about the use of wine and all drinks that have alcohol in them: "Wine is a mocker and beer a brawler; whoever is led astray by them is not wise" (Proverbs 20:1).

"Who has woe? Who has sorrow? Who has strife? Who has complaints? Who has needless bruises? Who has bloodshot eyes? Those who linger over wine, who go to sample bowls of mixed wine. Do not gaze at wine when it is red . . . ! In the end it bites like a snake and poisons like a viper" (Proverbs 23:29-32).

Here are more precious gems of wisdom, on all sorts of subjects:

"A gossip betrays a confidence, but a trustworthy man keeps a secret" (Proverbs 11:13).

"A generous man will prosper" (Proverbs 11:25).

"He who wins souls is wise" (Proverbs 11:30).

"The Lord detests lying lips, but he delights in men who are truthful" (Proverbs 12:22).

WISDOM OF THE WISE

"A gentle answer turns away wrath, but a harsh word stirs up anger" (Proverbs 15:1).

"Pride goes before destruction, a haughty spirit before a fall" (Proverbs 16:18).

"Better a patient man than a warrior" (Proverbs 16:32).

"Friends always show their love. What are brothers for if not to share trouble?" (Proverbs 17:17, TEV).

"A cheerful heart is good medicine" (Proverbs 17:22).

"A man of many companions may come to ruin, but there is a friend who sticks closer than a brother" (Proverbs 18:24).

"Even a child is known by his actions, by whether his conduct is pure and right" (Proverbs 20:11).

"A good name is more desirable than great riches; to be esteemed is better than silver or gold" (Proverbs 22:1).

"Train a child in the way he should go, and when he is old he will not turn from it" (Proverbs 22:6).

"Wounds from a friend can be trusted" (Proverbs 27:6).

"He who conceals his sins does not prosper, but whoever confesses and renounces them finds mercy" (Proverbs 28:13).

It would be good for you to memorize all these proverbs. Anyone who tries to follow their good advice will live a happy, prosperous life, because this is not merely the wisdom of Solomon—it is also the wisdom of God.

---
*1 Kings 4:32.

Solomon's Big Stumbling Block

(1 Kings 11:1-11)

GREAT, wise, and rich though he was, Solomon had one big stumbling block in his life. You will find it in the first verse of chapter 11 in the first book of Kings. "King Solomon, however, loved many foreign women."

He had many, many wives. Hundreds of them. So many, in fact, that he could hardly have remembered all their names. The worst of it was that these women were not Israelites, but "Moabites, Ammonites, Edomites, Sidonians, and Hittites," the very women God had expressly forbidden His people to marry.

Perhaps one reason why Solomon married so many wives was that each one brought with her a big dowry from a wealthy father. But though his wives brought him great riches, they "led him astray."

As a young man, he began his reign with his heart set on God. That's why he built the Temple and prayed that wonderful prayer of dedication. But when the foreign princesses came

162

flocking into Jerusalem, they wanted to worship their own gods. They didn't know any better.

Some of Solomon's wives were followers of "Ashtoreth, the goddess of the Sidonians," others of Molech, "the detestable god of the Ammonites." To please them and keep them happy and peaceful, Solomon built places of worship for these heathen gods.

"He did the same for all his foreign wives, who burned incense and offered sacrifices to their gods."

The good people of Jerusalem must have been shocked. To think that their king, the son of David, should permit such idolatry within sight of the beautiful Temple! It was awful!

The worship of Molech called for the sacrifice of living children. How could Solomon, who had shown such tenderness toward a baby when the two women came to him, now permit such horrible torture of innocent little ones? How far could a man fall?

No wonder "the Lord became angry with Solomon." He had reason to be. Twice He had appeared to the king in his younger days with promises of great blessing if he would do right and follow the ways of God. Now Solomon had failed Him. In

spite of all the wisdom the Lord had given him, he had allowed himself to become a fool. "Solomon did not keep the Lord's command," and soon began to pay the price of his disobedience and folly.

"So the Lord said to Solomon, 'Since this is your attitude and you have not kept my covenant and my decrees, which I commanded you, I will most certainly tear the kingdom away from you and give it to one of your subordinates.' "

How sad! How terribly sad! He had started out so well, and God had blessed him so greatly! Now he was rejected, just as Saul had been before him.

He had gained riches, power, prestige, everything a man could wish for, but he had forgotten God. And in losing God he had lost everything.

Is there a stumbling block in your life? Is there something that could cause you to forget God? Could someone look at you and say, "This boy has a nice home, many fine toys, a new bicycle, but he tells lies, or he doesn't think it is important to pray or go to church"?

Or could they say, "This girl has wonderful parents, beautiful clothes, the best of everything, but she is impatient, grumbles, and cares more about what her friends think than about what God says is right"?

Let's beware of the stumbling blocks in our lives.

PART FOUR

Stories of
Israel and Judah

(1 Kings 12:1-16:34)

The Price of Foolishness

(1 Kings 11:14-40)

WHAT a price there was to pay for Solomon's foolishness. The foreign princesses he invited into his palace not only brought their idols and their false religions with them, but they brought a lot of trouble, too.

When the people of Israel saw their famous king allowing such things to happen in Jerusalem, some of them naturally began to think that the gods of the heathen couldn't be so bad after all. If Solomon the Wise thought they were all right, what could be wrong with them? So idolatry began to spread through the land, and it took such a hold on the people's hearts that for hundreds of years nobody was able to get rid of it.

As the people gradually turned away from God, He turned away from them. He withdrew His blessings, and their lives grew dark, as when the sun goes behind a cloud.

The kingdom of Israel had been at peace from the river Euphrates to the border of Egypt, but now revolutions began to break out, first in one place, then in another. One was led by

167

The prophet Ahijah took off his beautiful new garment, tore it into twelve pieces, and gave ten of them to Jeroboam to show that God had made him ruler over the ten tribes of Israel.

Hadad the Edomite, and another by Rezon, the ruler of Aram, who "was Israel's adversary as long as Solomon lived." Then Jeroboam, one of Solomon's most trusted servants, turned against him.

One day as Jeroboam was walking alone in a field near Jerusalem, the prophet Ahijah met him, wearing a brand-new cloak.

To Jeroboam's surprise, Ahijah took off his new cloak, tore it into 12 pieces, and gave 10 of them to him. Then the prophet said, "Take ten pieces for yourself, for this is what the Lord, the God of Israel, says: 'See, I am going to tear the kingdom out of Solomon's hand and give you ten tribes. . . . They have forsaken me and worshiped Ashtoreth the goddess of the Sidonians, Chemosh the god of the Moabites, and Molech the god of the Ammonites, and have not walked in my ways, nor done what is right in my eyes, nor kept my statutes and laws as David, Solomon's father, did. . . . However, as for you, I will take you, and you will . . . be king over Israel."

This is something to think about. Solomon had all those wives, and, no doubt many children, but God hadn't chosen one of them. He gave 10 of the 12 tribes to a servant! How very displeased He must have been at the way Solomon had failed Him!

When Solomon heard that Ahijah had told Jeroboam that the Lord had chosen him to be king, Solomon tried to kill Jeroboam. "But Jeroboam fled to Egypt, to Shishak the king,

168

and stayed there until Solomon's death."

As the aging king saw his friends deserting him and all the trouble his wives had brought him, he began to see what a dreadful failure he had made of everything.

Looking back over his life, he said, "I undertook great projects: I built houses for myself and planted vineyards. I made gardens and parks and planted all kinds of fruit trees in them. I made reservoirs to water groves of flourishing trees. I bought male and female slaves and had other slaves who were born in my house. I also owned more herds and flocks than anyone in Jerusalem before me. I amassed silver and gold for myself, and

169

the treasure of kings and provinces. I acquired men and women singers, and a harem as well—the delights of the heart of man.

"I became greater by far than anyone in Jerusalem before me. In all this my wisdom stayed with me. I denied myself nothing my eyes desired; I refused my heart no pleasure. My heart took delight in all my work, and this was the reward for all my labor.

"Yet when I surveyed all that my hands had done and what I had toiled to achieve, everything was meaningless, a chasing after the wind; nothing was gained under the sun." [1]

And all because somewhere along life's journey, he had left God out.

Toward the end Solomon found God again and was sorry for all his mistakes. "Here is the conclusion of the matter," he wrote: "Fear God and keep his commandments, for this is the whole duty of man. For God will bring every deed into judgment, including every hidden thing, whether it is good or evil." [2]

But by the time Solomon found God again, it was too late to stop the consequences of his misdeeds. What a pity he did not follow this good advice all his life! How different everything would have been for him and for Israel!

---

[1] Ecclesiastes 2:4-11.
[2] Ecclesiastes 12:13, 14.

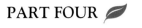

The Kingdom Divided

(1 Kings 11:42-12:30; 2 Chronicles 9:31-12:1)

WHEN Solomon died, he was buried in the City of David, "and Rehoboam his son succeeded him as king."

The coronation of the new king was to take place in Shechem, where there was plenty of room for thousands of people to gather for the great event. "All the Israelites" went there to make him king.

Meanwhile, news of Solomon's death had reached Jeroboam in Egypt. Remembering what the prophet Ahijah had said to him, Jeroboam hurried northward to see what would happen next.

When he arrived at Shechem everybody recognized him, for he had been one of Solomon's best-known and most efficient officers before he had fled to the court of Pharaoh. Many must have wondered why he had come back so soon after the old king's death. Few suspected that he would soon be the leader of a great rebellion.

After the coronation Jeroboam and some of the leaders of

171

Israel went to the new king and begged him to ease the burdens Solomon had given the people to bear. To support his great building program Solomon had taxed the people heavily and forced tens of thousands of people to work for him, whether they wanted to or not. Jeroboam and the other leaders wanted taxes reduced and the compulsory service laws abolished.

Rehoboam said he would let them know in three days. He talked the matter over with his older counselors, and they advised him to do what the leaders wanted. "If you will be kind to these people and please them and give them a favorable answer," they said, "they will always be your servants."

Not too sure of himself, Rehoboam turned to the younger men around him and asked what they thought he should do. They told him, in effect, to let the people see "who's boss" and rule with a heavy hand, right from the start.

Foolishly, Rehoboam "rejected the advice the elders gave him" and listened to the young men. He told the leaders of Israel, "My father made your yoke heavy; I will make it even heavier. My father scourged you with whips; I will scourge you with scorpions."

As the report of Rehoboam's answer spread among the thousands gathered in Shechem, everybody became very angry. They had come to the coronation hoping for relief, not for heavier burdens. They had put up with a

lot from Solomon, but they were not going to take it from this young upstart.

Suddenly the spirit of revolt flashed from heart to heart, spreading like wildfire through the camp. "What share do we have in David, what part in Jesse's son?" cried the men from the northern tribes. " 'To your tents, O Israel! Look after your own house, O David!' So all the Israelites went home."

The great rebellion was on.

Ten tribes followed Jeroboam and made him their king. Rehoboam was left with only two tribes, Judah and Benjamin.

When Rehoboam returned to Jerusalem, he was very upset. He saw what a dreadful mistake he had made. Because of his foolish speech he had lost most of his father's kingdom, and he wanted to get it back again. So he called up all his best soldiers, 180,000 men, and prepared to force the rebels to return.

Just then a man of God named Shemaiah brought him this message: "Do not go up to fight against your brothers. Go home, every one of you, for this is my doing."

It is to Rehoboam's credit that he obeyed the Lord's messenger and told his soldiers to go back home. Then he decided to make the best of things as they were and fortified many of the cities he had left, in case the rebels tried to take them away from him. "He strengthened their defenses and put commanders in them, with supplies of food, olive oil and wine. He put shields and spears in all the cities, and made them very strong. So Judah and Benjamin were his."

Meanwhile as the new king of the 10 tribes of Israel, Jeroboam began to reveal the kind of man he really was. As soon as he was king he set up two golden calves for the people to worship. The excuse he made was " 'It is too much for you to go up to Jerusalem. Here are your gods, O Israel, who brought you up out of Egypt.' One he set up in Bethel, and the other in Dan."

Then he offered sacrifices to these idols and "appointed priests from all sorts of people." He told the Levites they were not needed anymore, so they left their homes and went to Jerusalem.

Within five years of Solomon's death his proud, rich empire was torn apart, and the people were worshiping idols. The glory of Solomon's kingdom had vanished.

When Solomon married those heathen princesses he never dreamed all this would happen. He thought he was strong enough and wise enough to stand against their false religions. But he wasn't. His wives had won. First they stole his heart and then his kingdom.

Solomon's Temple Raided

(2 Chronicles 11:16-12:12)

FOR THREE years all went well with Rehoboam. Priests and Levites whose homes had been on land that was now part of the 10-tribe kingdom came flocking into Jerusalem, together with many others "who set their hearts on seeking the Lord, the God of Israel."

Shocked by all that had happened, the people prayed and worshiped as they had not done for a long time. For a while it seemed as though there might be a real revival. "They strengthened the kingdom of Judah and supported Rehoboam son of Solomon three years, walking in the ways of David and Solomon during this time."

But that was about the end of it, for Rehoboam had the same weakness as his father. He married many wives and soon he too forgot God.

"After Rehoboam's position as king was established and he had become strong, he and all Israel with him abandoned the law of the Lord."

For the next two years both Rehoboam and the people

175

drifted further and further from God. Then news reached them that Shishak, king of Egypt, was marching against them with an army of 60,000 horsemen and 1,200 chariots.

While Solomon was alive nobody had dared to attack the Hebrew nation, now the country's defense was not as strong. The Egyptians easily took all the cities Rehoboam had fortified so carefully, and they marched on Jerusalem.

"Then the prophet Shemaiah came to Rehoboam and to the leaders of Judah who had assembled in Jerusalem for fear of Shishak, and he said to them, 'This is what the Lord says, "You have abandoned me; therefore, I now abandon you to Shishak." ' "

The king and the leaders of Judah were startled. They had never thought that God might desert *them*, though they had forgotten *Him*. Falling to their knees, they confessed their sins and cried, "The Lord is in the right" (NRSV).

Always merciful, the Lord said to Shemaiah, "Since they have humbled themselves, I will not destroy them but will soon give them deliverance. My wrath will not be poured out on Jerusalem through Shishak."

SOLOMON'S TEMPLE RAIDED

Shishak had heard about the wealth of Solomon, and he wanted to see it for himself. He attacked Jerusalem, and forced his way in through the city's gates. Going straight to the beautiful Temple, he ransacked the place and "carried off the treasures of the temple of the Lord and the treasures of the royal palace. He took everything, including the gold shields Solomon had made."

Satisfied with all this loot, he did not destroy the Temple or the city, but went back home gloating over his good fortune in getting so much so easily.

When Shishak and his men were gone, Rehoboam and the princes of Judah went to the Temple to see what the raiders had left. How sad they must have been as they walked around the plundered building that once had been the glory of Israel and the envy of the world!

Rehoboam made shields of bronze to replace Solomon's shields of gold. That in itself tells the story of what had happened to the children of Israel and how poor they had become—because once more they had turned away from God.

The Broken Altar

(1 Kings 13:1-6)

WICKED though Jeroboam was, God had not completely turned away from him. One day as he worshiped before the golden calf which he had set up at Bethel he heard someone shouting. Turning to see who had dared to interrupt him, he saw a man dressed as a prophet of God.

The man was crying, "O altar, altar! This is what the Lord says: 'A son named Josiah will be born to the house of David. On you he will sacrifice the priests of the high places who now make offerings here, and human bones will be burned on you.' "

Jeroboam was furious. The man must be mad! How could he know the name of someone who hadn't been born yet, or what that person would do to this altar?

Not for a moment did the king realize that he was being given a glimpse into the future—300 years later—when good king Josiah would break down this very altar and grind

179

←— PAINTING BY KREIGH COLLINS

When Jeroboam heard the prophecy concerning Josiah and threatened to take the prophet's life, his arm became withered, and God destroyed the altar before his very eyes.

it "to powder." God was speaking, but Jeroboam did not know it. He was so angry he wanted to kill the prophet.

But the man of God went on. "This is the sign the Lord has declared," he said. "The altar will be split apart and the ashes on it will be poured out."

This was too much for Jeroboam.

He pointed to the prophet of God. "Seize him!" he cried. But the hand Jeroboam "stretched out toward the man shriveled up, so that he could not pull it back."

At the same moment the altar he had been holding onto split apart, the ashes on it pouring down the cracks. He was frightened now, and he had good reason to be.

"Pray for me!" he cried.

The prophet prayed, and God, in His great mercy, healed Jeroboam, despite all the wrong he had done. "The king's hand was restored and became as it was before."

This was Jeroboam's last chance to repent and change his life. Did he take it? Did he break down his idols and bring the 10 tribes back to God? He did not. Instead he led them deeper into sin. The Bible says, "Even after this, Jeroboam did not change his evil ways."

Killed by a Lion

(1 Kings 13:7-30)

"COME home with me . . . ," Jeroboam said to the prophet, "and I will give you a gift."

"No," said the man of God. "Even if you were to give me half your possessions, I would not go with you, nor would I eat bread or drink water here."

"Why not?" asked Jeroboam.

"Because," he replied, "I was commanded by the word of the Lord: 'You must not eat bread or drink water or return by the way you came.' "

So the prophet went back home.

Some boys had seen what had happened to Jeroboam and the altar. Now they rushed home to their old father to tell him the news. I can almost hear them saying, "Dad, you should have seen the king's face when he found his arm withered and saw the altar break in pieces!"

"Which way did the prophet go?" the old man asked, anxious to learn more about what had happened. They told him.

"Saddle my donkey," he said, and they did. Riding as fast

181

as he could, he hurried after the man of God. He finally found him sitting under an oak.

"Come home with me and eat," he said to him.

"No, thanks," said the man of God, telling him just what he had told Jeroboam.

Then the old man lied to him. "I too am a prophet, as you are," he said. "And an angel said to me by the word of the Lord: 'Bring him back with you to your house so that he may eat bread and drink water.' "

Deceived, the man of God went back with him. As soon as he finished his supper, however, the old man said to him, "This is what the Lord says: 'You have defied the word of the Lord and have not kept the command the Lord your God gave you. . . . Therefore your body will not be buried in the tomb of your fathers.' "

At once the man of God knew he had made a dreadful mistake. Sadly he got on the donkey that the old man gave him and rode away.

Not far along the road "a lion met him . . . and killed him."

Other travelers passing by saw the dead man with a lion and a donkey standing beside him. They hurried to the city where the old man lived and told their strange story. The old man went out to see if it was true. It was.

There was the lion, the donkey, and the body of the man of God. "The lion had neither eaten the body nor mauled the donkey." So the old man put the body on the donkey, brought it home, and buried it in his own tomb, saying, "Oh, my brother!"

What a lesson for us! How careful we must be! This man

was wonderfully honored by God when he stood before Jeroboam. He saw the altar split apart and the king's arm wither. He even saw his prayer for the king answered instantly. Since God had clearly spoken through him, the prophet should not have been so quick to believe the old man's false message, which was so different from what God had given him.

He could easily have asked God if there had been any change in His instructions. Instead, like Eve in the Garden of Eden, the man of God thoughtlessly allowed himself to believe a lie.

And since the prophet had just delivered this serious message about the results of disobedience, he should have been especially careful to obey God's distinct instructions for his own behavior. The eyes of the whole country, and especially the king, were on him. But 24 hours later he was dead, killed by a lion, because he had not trusted God and had openly disobeyed Him. God could not let the important lesson of obedience that the prophet had been teaching the king be ruined by the prophet's own disobedience.

Queen in Disguise

(1 Kings 14:1-18)

NOT LONG after the prophet's warning to Jeroboam, a great sorrow came to the king's home. His son Abijah became sick, and nobody could do anything for him.

At last Jeroboam remembered the prophet Ahijah, who had told him years before that he would someday be king over the 10 tribes of Israel. Jeroboam believed that Ahijah could make the boy well, if he wanted to. But would he? Not if he knew who the boy really was. That fact must be kept from him at all costs.

Jeroboam told his wife to disguise herself and go to Shiloh, where Ahijah was living. "Take ten loaves of bread with you, some cakes and a jar of honey, and go to him. He will tell you what will happen to the boy."

By this time Ahijah was old and blind, so that there was no need for the queen to disguise herself. But she did anyway, thinking she could deceive the prophet of the Lord. How mistaken she was! He knew her at once. To her great amazement,

as Ahijah "heard the sound of her footsteps at the door," he said to her, "Come in, wife of Jeroboam."

Too startled to speak, the queen never said a word. All she could do was listen to the words of doom the aged prophet spoke to her.

"Go, tell Jeroboam," Ahijah said to her, "that this is what the Lord, the God of Israel, says: 'I raised you up from among the people and made you a leader over my people Israel. I tore the kingdom away from the house of David and gave it to you, but you have not been like my servant David. . . . You have made for yourself other gods, idols made of metal; you have provoked me to anger and thrust me behind your back.

185

" 'Because of this, I am going to bring disaster on the house of Jeroboam.' "

As for Jeroboam's child, there was no hope. He would die. But because God saw some good in him, he only, of all Jeroboam's children, would be buried in a grave.

Ahijah had an equally grim message for the 10 tribes which Jeroboam had led into sin. "The Lord," he said, "will uproot Israel from this good land that he gave to their forefathers and scatter them beyond the [Euphrates] River, because they provoked the Lord to anger by making Asherah poles."

When Ahijah had finished speaking the queen went sadly on her way, wondering how she would tell her husband what he had said to her.

When she arrived at "the threshold of the house," her child died. She knew then that all the other dreadful things Ahijah had told her would come true.

You would think that all this would have been enough to turn Jeroboam from his evil ways. But it was not. Like Pharaoh long before, Jeroboam hardened his heart again. He plunged from one sin into another until there was no hope for him or for his kingdom.

Grandmother's Idol

(1 Kings 15:1-14; 2 Chronicles 13:1-15:17)

DOWN south in the kingdom of Judah, King Rehoboam died. In his place reigned his son Abijah, whose mother Maacah, had been Rehoboam's favorite wife.

Maacah was Absalom's granddaughter and David's great-granddaughter. She had become interested in the heathen religions that Solomon's wives had brought into Jerusalem and had begun to worship the idols they had set up. Worse still, she taught her son these evil things so that "he committed all the sins his father had done before him; his heart was not fully devoted to the Lord his God."

However, he was not altogether bad. One day he was attacked by a vast army led by Jeroboam. Defeat seemed certain. But Abijah called out to Jeroboam and his soldiers, "As for us, the Lord is our God, and we have not forsaken him. . . . God is with us; he is our leader. His priests with their trumpets will sound the battle cry against you." Defeat was turned into victory.

187

Soon after that, Abijah died, having reigned only three years. Then Asa came to the throne, and he "did what was good and right in the eyes of the Lord his God. He removed the foreign altars and the high places, smashed the sacred stones and cut down the Asherah poles."

Just who trained Asa we are not told, but it certainly wasn't his grandmother. She continued to worship her own private idol until one day, when Asa was strong enough, he "deposed his grandmother Maacah from her position as queen mother, because she had made a repulsive Asherah pole. Asa cut the pole down, broke it up and burned it in the Kidron Valley" just outside Jerusalem.

It must have taken a lot of courage to burn his grand-mother's idol, but God was pleased with him for doing it, and He blessed him in many ways.

One day the Cushites came up against Judah "with a vast army and three hundred chariots. Asa was alarmed, but he cried to God, saying, "There is no one like you to help the powerless against the mighty. Help us, O Lord our God, for we rely on you, and in your name we have come against this vast army. O Lord, you are our God; do not let man prevail against you."

In answer to this beautiful prayer, God struck down the Cushites and they fled. "Such a great number of Cushites fell that they could not recover."

Not long after this King Asa was met by the prophet Azariah, son of Obed, who said to him, " 'The Lord is with you when you are with him. If you seek him, he will be found by you, but if you forsake him, he will forsake you. . . . Be strong and do not give up, for your work will be rewarded.'

"When Asa heard these words, . . . he took courage." He destroyed all the "detestable idols" in Judah and Benjamin.

For 41 years Asa reigned in Jerusalem. He was one of the best kings Judah ever had. He made some mistakes, of course, but his heart "was fully committed to the Lord all his life." And that's a wonderful thing for God to say about anybody.

From Bad to Worse

(1 Kings 15:25-16:33)

THINGS were going from bad to worse in the northern kingdom of Israel. After Jeroboam died, his son Nadab took the throne. But he was as bad as his father, and "did evil in the eyes of the Lord."

Nadab didn't last long—barely two years. Then a man named Baasha rebelled against him, killed him, and took his throne. To make sure that none of Jeroboam's other sons would try to take the kingdom away from him, Baasha "killed Jeroboam's whole family. He did not leave Jeroboam anyone that breathed," just as Ahijah the prophet had said would happen.

Baasha reigned 24 years, but he wasn't any better than Jeroboam. "He did evil in the eyes of the Lord," even though God did send the prophet Jehu to warn him of what would happen to him if he refused to change his ways.

When Baasha died, his son Elah came to the throne and reigned two years. He was a drunkard, and Zimri, commander of half the king's chariots, plotted against him and killed him.

Zimri made himself king, but he held the throne only seven days. While he was busy killing all the relatives of Baasha, the people of Israel made Omri king.

Omri and his men marched on the capital city of Tirzah, where Zimri was living, and captured it. "When Zimri saw that the city was taken, he went into the citadel of the royal palace and set the palace on fire around him. So he died."

That was the end of Zimri, but Omri's troubles were not over yet. Another man named Tibni wanted to be king, and half of the people supported him. So there was more fighting until "Tibni died and Omri became king."

Omri was king for 12 years. During his reign he did one

thing of great importance. He bought a hill for two talents of silver (150 pounds, or 70 kilograms) and built a city on it. He called this city Samaria and moved his capital there.

It was a great chance to start all over again. Everything was new and clean and beautiful. All that was evil, all that belonged to the bad old days, could have been left behind. Yet while two talents of silver could buy a hill, they could not make it holy. They could buy houses and lands, and maybe a new palace for the king, but they could not buy peace and righteousness. Something more was needed for that, and nobody had it.

When Omri died, Ahab his son reigned in his place. "He not only considered it trivial to commit the sins of Jeroboam son of Nebat, but he also married Jezebel daughter of Ethbaal king of the Sidonians, and began to serve Baal and worship him. He set up an altar for Baal in the temple of Baal that he built in Samaria. Ahab . . . did more to provoke the Lord, the God of Israel, to anger than did all the kings of Israel before him."

So, just 62 years after the death of Solomon the people of Israel had completely turned their backs on God. Their king was an idolater, their queen a heathen, and their capital city boasted a temple to Baal. Things could not have been much worse. The stage was set for the coming of Elijah the prophet.